Little Visits With God

LITTLE VISITS

Devotions for Families

Publishing House
St. Louis

WITH GOD

with Grade School Children

By ALLAN HART JAHSMANN

and MARTIN P. SIMON

Illustrations by FRANCES HOOK

MANUFACTURED IN THE UNITED STATES OF AMERICA

45 46 47   93 92

Foreword

Here, indeed, is a unique book of devotions for families with young children. While involving their interest and participation, it also offers rich instruction for older children and adults.

There is nothing routine and formal about these devotions. They are full of warmth, dipped right out of life. Those of us whose children are grown could almost wish them young again in order to share these readings with them.

This book will help children not only to know about God, but also to love Him and to trust in Him. It cultivates right attitudes and shows how the Christian faith is to function in daily living. These devotions touch the heart as well as reach the mind. They are childlike without being childish. They lead to Jesus, the Savior and Good Shepherd. And it is through childlike trust in Jesus that we are saved.

The authors are to be congratulated on their achievement, rarely equaled in the devotional literature I have seen. The church has produced many prayer books for small children. This is one of the first devotional books to capture the interest of the child along with the parent and to relate this interest to a discussion of the truths of Christian faith and life.

The authors represent a fine combination of talents united in a common task. Martin P. Simon, editor of the *Christian Parent* magazine, has long been known for his ability to draw illustrations from everyday life. Allan Hart Jahsmann is a specialist in Sunday school materials for small children. He is the author of *Teaching Little Amalee Jane* and knows her brother Johnny, too.

It is a distinct pleasure to help send this book on its way into the hearts and homes of Christian parents and into the lives of their children. By using these devotions early in life, parents will sow seeds that will enrich all the years to come. Worship periods in the home produce God-fearing people who are also a blessing to others. May the church have many families who meet with God daily in family worship.

OSCAR E. FEUCHT

Authors' Note

The language used in these devotions was determined largely by a concern for the child. This accounts for the frequent use of popular though sometimes "incorrect" grammar, and the simplification of some of the Bible verses. Brief life-experience stories have been related in order to make the devotional reading more interesting and meaningful. Parents will provide a happy learning situation if they will regularly take time to visit with God as a family — either at the breakfast or supper table or in a family circle at the children's bedtime hour. Older children will enjoy reading this book personally. The discussion questions are for informal conversation, and a hymn may precede or follow the reading. May the Holy Trinity be pleased with the book, and may all who use it be enriched as they commune with God and learn to follow their Savior Jesus more faithfully every day in every way.

A. H. J.
M. P. S.

Contents

x

*Blessed is he whose sin
is forgiven.* Psalm 32:1

Why We Can Always Be Happy

Jerry wasn't happy. When his father came home from work, Jerry hurried upstairs. His mother had to call him four times before he came down to supper.

At the table his father asked, "Who broke the window in the garage?" Jerry said nothing, but he felt his face get hot. "You played ball over there, didn't you?" said his father. "And we told you not to."

Jerry looked at his plate and still said nothing. He could hardly swallow the bread he was chewing. Then he began to cry.

"I'm sorry," he said. "I'll pay for it from my allowance. And I won't play ball there again. I promise."

His parents were glad to hear Jerry talk that way. He was sorry he had done wrong. And he promised to do better. "All right, Jerry," said his father softly, "we'll forget it. God forgives you when you're sorry, so we will, too. But please don't disobey us again."

Next morning Jerry whistled as he walked to school. He was happy now. God had put joy into his heart. "I wonder why it feels so good to be forgiven," he thought. "Thank You, God," he said, "for always being willing to forgive us."

Let's talk about this: Why didn't Jerry want to see his father? What wrong had Jerry done? Was it easy for Jerry to say, "I'm sorry"? Why did Jerry feel so good the next day? The Bible says, "Be glad in the Lord . . . and shout for joy," because God forgives us our sins every day for Jesus' sake.

Older children and grownups may now read: Psalm 32:8-11.

Let us pray together: Dear Lord, we're glad that we can come to You at any time and can always receive forgiveness. Keep us from doing wrong, make us sorry for our sins, and help us to believe in Jesus, our Savior. Then we shall always be happy children of God. We ask this in Jesus' name. Amen.

*All things were made
    by Jesus.* John 1:3

What Jesus Made

Jim said, "My new wagon is scratched. I'll wait a few days; maybe it will get better." Will that wagon get fixed? Not by itself.

Bill said, "My hand is scratched. I'll put on a bandage; soon it will be better." Will that hand get better by itself? Yes, it probably will.

What's the difference? A man made the wagon. Jesus made the hand. The things which Jesus made are much more wonderful than anything a man can make.

What all did Jesus make? The Bible says that all things

in the beginning of the world were made by Him. Jesus made the sun and the moon and the stars. He made the lions and the cows. He made grass and trees begin to grow. He made the first people. "Without Him was not anything made that was made," says the Bible. What do you think of that?

When the world was made, God said to the first people, "You take care of the world and rule it." Jesus had put many wonderful things into the world for people to use in making things. He also gave people minds so they could figure out how to make things from what He had made.

But in the beginning all things were made by Jesus. And the things which Jesus made still can't be made by people. You see, Jesus is God, and God is much wiser and greater than the people He made.

Let's talk about this: Why can a hand fix itself while a wagon cannot? What are some of the things Jesus made? For whom did He make them? What did He give to people so that they could make things from what He had made? What must Jesus be if He made all things in the world?

Bible reading for older children and grownups: John 1:1-5.

Let us pray to Jesus: What a wonderful world You have made for us, Lord Jesus. All that You have made shows Your great power and love. We are glad that You made us and that You also saved us when we became spoiled by sin. Make and keep us all as God's children by giving us the Holy Spirit. Amen.

Not Seen, But Loved

"Mother, how does Jesus look?" asked Winifred. Her aunt had given her a picture of Jesus for her birthday, and it didn't look like the other pictures of Jesus at all. That's why she asked, "How does Jesus look?"

Her mother couldn't tell her. "I don't know, Honey," she said, "and nobody else knows either. They didn't make a picture of Him when He lived on earth. The pictures we see are just the way some painters thought He may have looked."

"You mean," said Winifred, "all the pictures are just make-believe pictures of Jesus?"

"That's right," said her mother; "that's the best we have. Nobody really knows how Jesus looked. Do you think you can still love Him even if you don't know how He looked?" asked Winifred's mother with a smile.

"Oh, sure," said Winifred. "I love Him no matter how He looks. But I'd like to know."

"You make me think of a little Bible verse," said Winifred's mother. "The verse says, 'Without having seen Jesus, you love Him.' That's what Peter wrote to all of God's children long ago."

"You know why, Mother? Because we know what He did for us," said Winifred. "That's why we love Him without knowing how He looks."

Let's talk about this: What did Winifred wonder one day? Who does Jesus look like? How do you think Jesus looks? Why doesn't anybody really know? Why do we love Jesus even though we have never seen Him?

4

Bible reading for older children and grownups: 1 Peter 1:3-9.

Let us pray together: We would love You, dear Jesus, no matter how You looked. We love You because You loved us and died on a cross to save us. Keep us from sin and someday take us to heaven, where we will see You and be with You forever. Amen.

Serve the Lord
  with gladness. Psalm 100:2

Service with a Smile

"What's Ella doing?" asked Mr. James.

"She's helping Mother," said Fred.

Mr. James went to the kitchen to see how Ella was helping. She wasn't helping very much. She had a face a mile long, and it was sour enough to can pickles.

"Well, well," said her daddy, "something must be wrong. My little girl isn't happy helping her mother, is she?"

"No," said Ella.

"O. K.," said her daddy, "I'll finish drying the dishes for you if you'll learn a little Bible verse for me."

That was fine with Ella. "Which Bible verse?" asked Ella when her daddy was finished with the dishes.

"It's in Psalm 100," said Mr. James. "That makes it easy to find in the Bible. Hunt up verse 2."

Ella found it and read, "Serve the Lord with gladness."

"How are we to serve the Lord?" asked her father, as though he didn't know.

"With gladness," said Ella. "Do I serve the Lord when I help Mother?"

5

"You can," said Mr. James. "But I'm afraid you didn't do it with gladness this time."

"I'm sorry," said Ella; "next time I'll try to smile. I want to please Jesus in what I do," she said. This made her father happy.

Let's talk about this: What was Ella doing? How did she show that she wasn't glad to do it? Who did it for her? Which Bible verse did he ask her to learn? Why did Ella want to serve the Lord Jesus with gladness?

Older children and grownups may now read: Psalm 100.

Let us pray together: Dear Lord Jesus, we are glad that You are our God and Savior and that we are Your children. Please help us to remember that we can serve You in whatever we do. Then even our work will become pleasant, and we will do it gladly. Amen.

God cares for you. 1 Peter 5:7

Let God Do Your Worrying

Billy was having his first ride in a big, fast bus. He was on his way to Grandma's with his daddy and mother. Billy was sitting up in front, where he could see ahead.

"Mother," he said, "down there the hills come together and the road stops. Where will we go?"

"Don't you worry," said his mother.

His father said, "Let the driver worry about that, Billy. He's been here before."

Everything turned out all right. When they got to the bottom of the hill, Billy found out that the road kept on going around a curve. Then they came to a big city with many streets and houses.

"Mother," said Billy, "how does the driver know on which street to drive? There are so many streets. What if he drives down a wrong street?"

"The driver knows what he is doing," said Billy's mother. "Let him do the worrying."

Billy was young and foolish, but even grown-up people often worry like that. Some say, "I'm afraid we won't have enough money when we are old." Others say, "I don't see how we can pay our doctor bill or how I am going to do all my work or how we can stand what is happening."

The Bible says, "God cares for you." This also means, "God worries for you." In a way He is like the bus driver if you are riding in His bus on the way to heaven. He knows the way, and He'll get you there safely. He'll also take care of you on the way. So why worry? Let God do your worrying for you.

Let's talk about this: Why did Billy worry on the bus? What did his mother and father tell him? Why do even older people worry sometimes? Who is willing to worry for us? Why? Let's say the Bible verse together.

Bible reading for older children and grownups: Psalm 23.

Let us pray: Dear Jesus, we thank You for being willing to do our worrying for us. Please forgive us when we do not trust in You. Help us to remember how much You love us so that we will not worry. Amen.

I will praise You, O Lord . . .
I will sing praises. Psalm 108:3

Singing Praises to God

Little Carol couldn't talk plainly, but she was singing at the top of her voice, "Dedud love me, did I know, fo da Biba tell me toe."

Do you know what she was singing? It doesn't matter. She was singing praises to God, and Jesus heard it and was pleased.

"I will sing praises to the Lord," said King David in Psalm 108. Almost every Christian boy or girl has done it, too. Why? Because in the Bible God has promised to love us and to help us and to keep us as His children for Jesus' sake. That makes us want to thank and praise God, doesn't it?

What is one of the best ways of praising the Lord? By singing hymns. In hymns we tell what God has done for us, and we thank Him for His wonderful love.

Here are some questions to ask yourself: How many hymns do I know? At home, in Sunday school, in the church service, or anywhere else, do I gladly join with others in singing hymns? Do I praise God when I sing hymns, or just move my lips and make some sounds?

In church, when you are waiting for the service to begin, turn to a hymn you enjoy, and learn part of it from memory. Learn more of it the next Sunday until you know it well. Then sing it at home, on the way to school, or at any time.

It is good to sing hymns to the Lord and to praise Him with singing. Those who know and love God say, "I will praise You, O Lord . . . I will sing praises to You."

Let's talk about this: What was little Carol singing? Why was God pleased? Who said, "I will sing praises to the

8

Lord"? Why do God's children enjoy singing hymns? Which hymns do we know well? How could we learn to know more hymns? Which hymn could we sing together right now?

Older children and grownups may now read: Psalm 108:1-5.

Prayer: Dear Lord, teach me to sing Your praises. Amen.

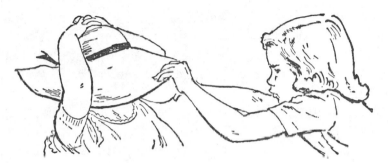

The earth is the Lord's and the fullness thereof. Psalm 24:1

What Do You Think You Own?

"This is mine, and you can't have it," said Loretta to Anne. They were playing dress-up. Loretta was wearing her mother's old dress, and she was reaching for a hat just when Anne grabbed it, too.

"It's mine," said Anne. "It's mine as much as yours."

They would have quarreled, but their mother stopped them.

"Whose hat did you say that was?" she asked.

The girls both giggled. "It's yours, Mother," they said.

"But didn't I hear you say that it was yours?" asked their mother.

"Oh, we were just saying that," said Loretta.

Then the mother sat down on the floor with them. "Do you know what this makes me think about?" she asked. "God gives us so many things: food to eat, clothes to wear, a house to live in, good health so that we can work, a mind that can think, a job for our daddy to earn money. He also gives us the wood and rubber and metal from which cars and TV's and everything else is made. But all things really belong to God."

Loretta understood what her mother was trying to teach her. "I know," she said, "people act as though things belonged to them, just the way we acted, but they really don't, do they? God could take away whatever He gives us, couldn't He?"

"Yes, He could," said her mother. "The Bible says, 'The earth is the Lord's and the fullness thereof.' Nothing that we have really belongs to us. It belongs to God. God just lets us have things to use and to enjoy for a while. And don't forget that He wants us to be good to other people with what He gives to us."

Let's talk about this: Whose hat did both girls want? Whose hat did they say it was? Why do people act as though things belonged to them? How many things really belong to us? Why does God let us have them? Can you say Psalm 24, verse 1?

Bible reading for older children and grownups: Psalm 50:10-15.

Let us pray together: Dear Father in heaven, please help us always to remember that all things in heaven and on earth belong to You and that we really don't own anything. Make us willing to use what You let us have for a while in ways that are pleasing to You. Keep us from ever becoming selfish by thinking that things belong to us. Make us thankful for Your gifts and willing to help other people with them. Amen.

Wash me, and I shall be whiter
than snow. Psalm 51:7

How to Get Clean Inside

"Did you wash your hands, Dick?" his mother asked. "Yes, I did," said Dick. But when he showed his hands to his mother, she said, "You didn't use soap, did you? And you didn't wash here and here and here." So Dick had to go and wash again. This time he tried to wash clean with soap.

There is a way in which boys and girls can get real clean the first time. When they let their mothers wash them, they usually get clean, at least on the outside.

But even mothers can't wash away the bad things that their children think and say and do. They can't wash their children's sins away. Only God can do that. When He forgives a person's sins, He washes them all away. That is why King David said in a psalm, "Wash me, and I shall be whiter than snow."

Mothers like to have their wash real white when it hangs on a line. White clothes with black marks on them are not clean and beautiful. Black marks on white clothes make most mothers unhappy.

When we are naughty, we sin. Sin is like a black spot on a clean white sheet. God wants His children to be clean on the inside. And we want to be clean and white for God inside. We want to be clean from sin even when our hands and clothes get dirty. Only a clean and decent person can be a child of God.

David said, "If God will wash me, then I will be perfectly clean from sin, whiter than snow." Sometimes snow is dirty, but when God washes us, we are whiter than snow. Not one speck of sin is left when God forgives us. Isn't that wonderful?

11

Let's talk about this: Who could have washed Dick cleaner than he washed himself? What could Dick's mother not wash away? Who alone can wash us on the inside? When God washes away sins, how many are left? How does God wash away our sins?

Bible reading for older children and grownups: Psalm 51:1-7.

Let us pray: Forgive us all our sins, dear God, so that we may be whiter than snow and holy in Your eyes. In Jesus' name we ask this. Amen.

Give thanks always
  for all things. Ephesians 5:20

Always Thank God!

"Do I have to go to school? Do I have to wash the dishes? Do I have to make my bed?" Kathy grumbled. Sometimes her mother would say, "Kathy, you're always grumbling."

"Well, what should I do?" asked Kathy, whining again.

"Jesus wants us always to be thankful for everything," said Kathy's mother.

"Always?" asked Kathy. "For everything?"

"That's what it says in the Bible," her mother told her. " 'Give thanks always for all things.' That's what it says."

"You mean," said Kathy, "I should thank God for having to wash the dishes and having to make my bed?"

"Well," said her mother, "there are people in other countries who never have many dirty dishes because they never have much to eat. There are some people who never have to make their beds because they have no beds; they are too poor."

"You mean," said Kathy, "when I wash the dishes I should thank God for the food that made the dishes dirty? And when I make my bed I should thank God for having a nice warm bed?"

"That's right, Honey," said her mother, "and a hundred other things like that. I hope you'll learn to 'give thanks for all things.' That will make you happy."

Let's talk about this: Why did Kathy often grumble and complain? What Bible verse did her mother teach her? For what can we thank God when we have dishes to wash? Why can we be thankful when we have a bed to make? Which person pleases Jesus, the one who is thankful or the one who whines often? Which person is happy, the grumbler or the one who is thankful?

Bible reading for older children and grownups: Ephesians 5:17-21.

Let us pray for a thankful heart: Dear Father in heaven, first help us to remember how much You love us. Help us also to believe that all things are just right for those who love You. Then make us thankful to You for all things so that we will always be Your happy children. We ask this in Jesus' name. Amen.

*Be followers of God, as {His}
dear children.* Ephesians 5:1

Following Our Leader

"Follow the leader!" said the boys and girls at Dixie's birthday party. Then Dixie led them up into the attic and down into the cellar and between the bushes outside and over a ditch.

When the children came in for a lunch, Dixie's father said to them, "You all are real good at following the leader. I didn't think little George would keep up with you." The children laughed.

"I know another way to play 'Follow the Leader,'" said Dixie's father.

"Let's play it," they all shouted.

"Well, maybe I shouldn't have said it was a game," he explained. "Christians are supposed to follow God as their Leader. When I saw you following the leader, I thought of a little Bible verse. I wrote it on a card for you to take home."

Everybody wanted a card. On it they read these words from the Bible: "Be followers of God." Little George couldn't read, so he asked Dixie to read his card for him.

"I follow Jesus," said George.

"Fine," said Dixie's father. "But Dixie led you over some places where it was hard to follow. Do you think it's easy to follow Jesus?" he asked the children.

"No," said one of the boys, "sometimes it's hard to be a good Christian. But it's fun trying to be one when you love Jesus."

"Good," said Dixie's father. "Do you know what Jesus wants His followers to do? The Bible says, 'Love, as Christ also has loved us.' We follow our Leader Jesus by loving."

14

Let's talk about this: What did the children play at the party? Why was it hard to follow Dixie? Which verse did her father write on cards for the children? What does Jesus expect His followers to do? Why isn't this easy?

Older children and grownups may now read: Ephesians 4:31—5:4.

Let us pray: Dear Lord Jesus, we have not always followed You as we should. Please forgive us. Help us to love people as You have loved us, even when this is hard to do. Amen.

*The eyes of the Lord are
in every place.* Proverbs 15:3

God Sees Everything

Who do you think was right, Jim or John?

Jim said, "I wish God didn't see everything. Then He wouldn't see what I do wrong."

John said, "I'm glad God sees everything. That's how He can help me all the time."

Both Jim and John had good reasons for what they said, but let's see who was right.

The Bible says, "The eyes of the Lord are in every place." They see the bad that we do and also the good. They see what we are thinking and whether or not we love Him and people. The eyes of the Lord see in the dark as well as in the light. They see us all the time.

Of course, we are all like Jim. We do many bad things and wish God could not see them. But we cannot run away from God; for He is everywhere. And we cannot hide anything from Him, because He sees everything.

There is only one way to hide our sins. We must let God hide them. When we ask God to forgive our sins for Jesus' sake, He covers them up and wipes them away. Because He forgives their sins, His children never have to be afraid of Him. Instead, we can be glad that He sees us in every place so that nothing can hurt us.

Let's talk about this: Where are the eyes of God? What does this mean? Why didn't Jim like that? Why was John happy that God's eyes are everywhere? Which is the only way to hide our sins from God? Why don't we ever have to be afraid of God seeing us? Why is it a good thing that the eyes of the Lord are in every place? Let us try to remember the Bible verse by saying it together.

Bible reading for older children and grownups: Psalm 139:1-12.

Let us also pray: Dear Lord God, we know that we cannot hide anything from You and that You know the truth about us all the time. Please forgive us all our sins for Jesus' sake so that we need not be afraid of what You see. Make us glad that You always see us and watch over us. Amen.

The very hairs of your head
    are all numbered. Matthew 10:30

God Counts Our Hairs

"How many children are there in the world, Daddy?" asked Sally.

"I don't know," said her daddy; "millions and millions of them."

"Then how can God take care of me?" asked Sally. "How

16

can He know where I am and what's happening to me? There are so many other boys and girls."

"Oh, God knows about you all right," said her dad. "He not only knows you; He knows how many hairs you have on your head. And He knows when one of them falls down. How many sparrows do you think there are in the world?" he asked.

Sally tried to think. "More sparrows than children, I guess," she said.

"Well, Jesus said that our Father in heaven cares for them all, and not one of them falls down dead unless He lets it fall. So if God takes care of every sparrow, don't you think He can take care of you, too?" asked Sally's dad.

"Sure," said Sally. "But I didn't know He counted my hairs," she said.

"He doesn't have to count them like you and I would," her daddy explained. "He knows everything, and he knows how many hairs we have without counting them. He also knows all about us and can take care of us. He will, too, if we want Him to. Jesus said, 'Don't worry. You are worth more than many sparrows.'"

Let's talk about God's care: What did Sally want to know? Why? What did Jesus say our Father in heaven knows about our hair? What never happens to sparrows unless God lets it happen? Who is worth more to God than many sparrows? Let's say the Bible verse together. Why did Jesus tell us these words?

Bible reading for older children and adults: Matthew 10:29-39.

Let us pray together: We thank You, dear Father in heaven, for loving us and watching over us. Help us to remember that You know all about us at all times and that nothing can happen to us unless You let it happen. Keep us from sin and every evil, for Jesus' sake. Amen.

Children, obey your parents in all things. Col. 3:20

How Jesus Obeyed for Us

Guess who was the only perfect boy who ever lived. It was Jesus. When His mother Mary asked Him to get some water for her, He gladly did it. Joseph was a carpenter. When he needed somebody to hold a board, Jesus did it. Jesus didn't grumble; He didn't disobey. He even noticed things He could do without being asked.

The Bible says, "Jesus was subject to them." That means He willingly obeyed His parents.

But didn't He ever play at all? Oh, yes. His parents gave Him time to play, and they had fun together with Him. It was a happy little home, down there in Nazareth. His parents were happy because Jesus obeyed them in all things.

Jesus is God. God doesn't have to obey people. But He had a special reason for obeying Mary and Joseph. He did all of the things God wants US to do. He did them for us so that we could be saved. He also showed us that God's children are to obey their parents in all things. If we love Jesus, we will want to obey our parents.

18

Let's talk about this: Can you say the Bible verse? Who was the best boy that ever lived? How well did He obey His parents? Why didn't Jesus really have to obey His parents? Why did He want to obey them? How well does He want us to obey *our* parents? Will children obey their parents when they try to be like Jesus?

Older children and grownups may now read: Colossians 3:20-25.

Let us ask Jesus to help us obey our parents: Dear Jesus, please forgive us for not always obeying our parents the way You did. Help us to become more like You by gladly doing whatever our parents want us to do. Amen.

Even a child is known
  by his doings. Proverbs 20:11

How Others Get to Know You

"That little boy over there looks like a very good boy," said Mr. Smith. Mr. Smith was talking to the owner of a store about different kinds of people.

"I'm not sure. Let's wait and see what he does," said Mr. Brown, the storekeeper.

So they watched the boy. Pretty soon he hit his mother because she wouldn't give him what he wanted. Then he walked away. When his mother asked him to come back, he wouldn't do it. When another boy was in his way, he gave him a push. He also took toys off a counter and put them back in a wrong place.

"Even a child is known by his doings," said Mr. Brown. "That's what the Bible says."

"That's true," said Mr. Smith. "You can know what kind

19

of person a child is by what he does. I no longer think that little boy is a very good boy. He has not learned to obey his parents or to be kind to other people, or to help take care of other people's things."

"Even a child is known by his doings." Jesus said something like that, too. He said, "By their fruits you will know them." By fruits He meant whatever a person would say and do.

It's easy to say that we love Jesus. But people can tell whether or not we really love Him by the way we act. Even a child is known by his doings. What does my behavior tell about me? Can others see that I am a Christian from the way I act? Those are questions which remind us to do the things Jesus would do. Then people will know that we belong to Him.

Let's talk about this: At first, what did Mr. Smith think about the boy in the store? How did he find out that the boy wasn't a good boy? Which Bible verse did Mr. Brown say to Mr. Smith? Jesus once said that you can know people by their fruits. What did He mean by fruits? If a person, even a child, says that he is good, but behaves badly, is he good or bad? How can a child show that he loves Jesus?

Bible reading for older children and grownups: Proverbs 20:11-13.

Let us pray together: Dear God, we are glad that You forgive us when we do wrong. But we want others to know that we are Your children so that they will love You, too. Please help us to do whatever is right and good so that people will know that we love Jesus. Amen.

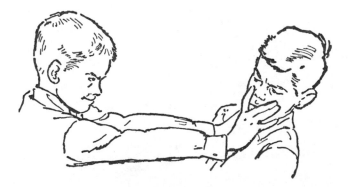

*With God nothing shall be
impossible.* Luke 1:37

God Can Do Anything

One winter some enemy soldiers were coming into a little town. In one of the houses near the town sat a little old grandmother. She was praying. "Dear God, please build a wall around us, and protect us from the soldiers," she prayed.

Her son heard her. He didn't believe in God. He said, "Mother, your God cannot build a wall around us in one night." But the little old grandmother kept right on praying.

The next morning her son could hardly believe what he saw. He couldn't look out of the windows. "Come here, Mother," he called. "God sent a snowstorm, and the wind has blown a big wall of snow against the house." Now the man believed that God can do anything and that He answers the prayers of His children. The soldiers had marched right past the house without even seeing it.

When God wants to do something for us, there isn't anything that can stop Him. Long ago God made the promise that He would send a Savior. He said the Savior would be His very own Son. When the Savior was ready to come, Mary was chosen to be His mother. God's own Son became a baby. He did this to save us all from sin. "With God nothing shall be impossible," says the Bible.

Let's talk about this: How many promises of God can you think of? Which of these promises has He kept? Which promises will God keep? When should we want God to keep His promises: when *He* thinks the time is right, or when *we* think so? What is the best way for God to answer our prayers: in *our* way or in the way which *He* thinks is best?

21

Older children and grownups may now read: Luke 1:26-38.

Let us thank God for His many wonderful promises: Dear God, thank You for the wonderful promises You have given us in the Bible. Thank You most of all for sending our Savior, as You promised You would. We are glad that You can do anything and that You always keep Your promises. Help us to trust You always, for Jesus' sake. Amen.

Thou shalt love the Lord, thy God . . .
   and thy neighbor as thyself. Luke 10:27

A Man Who Was Helpful

A man was riding along on a donkey. All of a sudden some robbers jumped out from behind a rock. They hit him over the head. They kept on beating him after he fell off the donkey. They took away all his money; also the other things he had. Then they ran away into the hills. They left the man lying by the side of the road. He was almost dead.

Two people who saw the poor man walked past him fast. They didn't want to help him. But then a kind stranger came by. He felt sorry for him. He stopped to see if he could help. He made bandages and tied up the man's wounds. He also put the man on his own donkey and took him to a hotel. He even paid somebody to take care of the man till he got better.

When we need help, wouldn't we want some good man to come by and help us? If somebody else needs help, Jesus said we are to be a good neighbor like the one who helped the man in the story. Then we will be loving our neighbor the way we love ourselves.

22

Let's talk about this: What happened to the man in the hills? What did two people do when they came that way? What did the third man do? Which man loved his neighbor? Did you ever help someone who needed help?

Older children and grownups may now read: Luke 10:30-37.

Let us pray together: Heavenly Father, please forgive us for doing so little for other people. Help us to know what to do for them, and make us glad to do it, for Jesus' sake. Amen.

I was glad when they said unto me, Let us go into the house of the Lord. Psalm 122:1

Are You Glad to Go to Church?

"Do I *have* to go to Sunday school and church?" asked Orville. His friends were going fishing. They had asked him to go along.

"Do I *have* to?" he asked again.

"Yes, Orville, you *have* to," said his father a little sadly. "But what can I do to make you say, 'I *want* to'?"

"It's a swell day for fishing," said Orville.

"It's also a swell day for hearing the Word of God," said his father. "Sunday is called the Lord's day. Every day

23

belongs to Him, but Sunday is one day on which good Christians go to their church regularly. And those who love the Lord Jesus more than anything else say what King David said long ago."

"What was that?" asked Orville.

"I was glad when they said unto me, Let us go into the house of the Lord."

"I'm glad to go to church," said Orville. "Only tomorrow I'd like to go fishing."

"I know how you feel," said his father. "It isn't that you don't want to go to church. I'm sure you would be very unhappy if our church were closed and we no longer had a place in which to worship God. But what if everybody went fishing tomorrow? Do you think there would be a church service?"

"No, I guess not," said Orville.

"What do you say we go fishing together in the afternoon?" asked his father.

"Oh, swell, Dad," said Orville. He really had wanted to go to church because he loved the Lord Jesus. Now he was glad he could go fishing, too.

Let's talk about this: Where did Orville want to go? Why did Orville's father say he *had* to go to church? What did King David say long ago in Psalm 122 when he thought of going to his church? What would Orville have loved more than God if he had gone fishing instead of to church? What is more important, fishing or visiting with God in His house? Let's learn to say the Bible verse from memory.

Older children and grownups may read: Luke 2:41-49.

Let us pray: We know how much we need to hear and learn Your Word, dear God. Please help us to love it, to understand it, to remember it, and to do it. Forgive us for not always loving You and Your house above all things, and make us glad to go to Your house whenever we can. Amen.

*Grow in grace and in knowing our Lord
and Savior Jesus Christ.* 2 Peter 3:18

Are You Growing as a Christian?

When Mary was not quite two years old, people would ask her, "How big are you?" Then Mary would raise her hands up high and say, "So big." Now Mary is grown up and never says that any more.

When our bodies are as tall as they can get to be, we say that we have stopped growing. But there are some ways in which we can keep on growing. Peter, the good friend of Jesus, says in our Bible verse, "Grow in grace and in knowing our Lord and Savior Jesus Christ."

What does it mean to "grow in grace"? What is grace, and how can we grow in it?

Grace is the wonderful love of God. Peter wants our faith in this love to grow and grow. To some other Christians St. Paul wrote, "We . . . thank God . . . that your *faith* is growing very much." *Faith* is believing that God loves us and that He forgives our sins and wants us to be His children. Peter wants us to learn to trust God's love more and more.

To grow in grace, we must grow in another way. We must learn to know Jesus better all the time. Only people who know Jesus know how good He is to them. That's why Peter also said we should grow in knowing our Lord.

Let's talk about this: When do people say they have stopped growing? What does our Bible verse tell us to keep growing in? What is grace? How can our faith in God's love keep on growing? In what ways can we learn more about Jesus?

Bible reading for older children and grownups: 2 Thessalonians 1:2-12.

Let us pray together: Dear Father in heaven, we want to keep on growing as Christians. Please help us to grow in grace by leading us to learn more about Jesus, our Lord and Savior. Amen.

The Lord is near to all them that call on Him. Psalm 145:18

Where God Is

What fun it was to go driving out to the mountains, far away from home! First Joe and his brother Gene counted the cars that passed. Then they raced to see which one could count 100 cows on his side of the road. Later they tried to be the first to see a white animal — a white horse or a cat or a cow or a dog. By evening they were many hundreds of miles away from home.

That night, as Joe lay in a cabin in a woods, something popped into his head and stayed right there. The more Joe thought about it, the more worried he became.

"Mother," said Joe, "how can we pray to God? He isn't 'way out here, is He?"

"Oh, yes, dear," she answered, "God is everywhere. We could go driving as long as we live, and God would still be there. There is no place where God is not. No matter where we are, God can hear our prayers."

"Is God nearby? Can He hear if I just whisper my prayers?" asked his brother Gene.

His mother smiled. "Yes," she said, "and you don't even have to whisper them. You can just think them, and God will hear your thoughts. The Bible says, 'The Lord is near to all them that call on Him.'"

So Gene and Joe prayed and went happily to sleep.

Let's talk about this: Why did little Joe think that God could not hear his prayers? Where is God? How loud must a prayer be for God to hear it? Can you say the Bible verse? To whom is God very near? How can we call on the Lord?

Older children and grownups may now read: Psalm 145:18-21.

Let us call on the Lord by praying: Thank You, dear Lord, for loving us and being kind and good to us. Please forgive us all our sins, and stay near us always, when we are at home or when we are away. We pray this in Jesus' name; we belong to Him. Amen.

Ask, and it shall be given you. Luke 11:9

Why Not Ask?

The apples on the tree in the neighbor's yard looked very good to Fred. But Fred knew that they did not belong to him. "I wish I could have some of those apples," said Fred to his father.

"Why don't you ask Mrs. Brown if you may have one?" said the father.

"I don't know," said Fred. He was bashful.

One day Mrs. Brown was walking past Fred's house. Fred said, "Your apples look very pretty, Mrs. Brown."

"Do they?" she said. "Would you like some?"

Fred nodded his head real fast. Yes, he would like some.

"Well, I'm glad you asked me," said Mrs. Brown. "You may go and pick some any time. But don't waste them."

Fred didn't wait long. He hurried over to Mrs. Brown's

yard to get some of the good apples. He could have had them sooner if only he had asked for them.

Did you know that we could have many more good things if we asked God for them? Jesus said, "Ask, and it shall be given you." Ask God for the things you need or would like. God listens when we pray, and God answers the prayers of His children. So let's not be afraid to ask God for many things. He loves us for Jesus' sake. He will give us whatever is good for us.

Let's talk about this: What did Fred wish he could have? What did Fred's father tell him to do? How did Mrs. Brown show that she loved Fred? Do you think that God loves His children as much as Mrs. Brown loved Fred? Suppose we asked for something that God did not want us to have; how would God answer our prayer then? What are some gifts that God is always willing to give us?

Older children and grownups may now read: Luke 11:5-10.

Let us pray together: Thank You, dear God, for telling us to ask You for whatever we want. Teach us to trust that You will give us what You know is best for us. Especially give us a strong faith in Jesus, our Savior, and fill our hearts with the Holy Spirit. We ask this in Jesus' name. Amen.

*God makes lightnings
for the rain.* Psalm 135:7

How Strong God Is!

One day little Jimmy noticed how strong his daddy was. When his mother couldn't open a jar of pickles, she called his daddy. He could open it. A little later his mother said, "I can't get the screen out of the window." But his daddy got it out easily. Then the faucet leaked, and his daddy fixed it.

The next day Jimmy ran over to play with Gordon. "My daddy is strong; he can do anything," Jimmy told Gordon. Did that make Jimmy afraid? No, it made him feel good.

When you hear thunder and see lightning, remember that it is God who makes the thunder roll and the lightning crack. Remember, too, that God is your Father in heaven. Your heavenly Father makes the lightnings for the rain, says the Bible.

Now, the next time you see God's lightning and hear His thunder, think about how strong and great God is. Jim said his father could do "anything." Jim was wrong. But our Father in heaven can do anything, anything He wants to do. And He wants to do only what is good for us. We are His children, and He loves us very much.

So, do we ever have to be afraid of lightning? Why, no. It shows us how strong and great our God is. Think of that when you see the lightning. And remember how wonderful it is that you are one of God's children.

Let's talk about this: When does God usually send lightning? Why are some people afraid of lightning? What does lightning tell us about God? Does God want to scare us with thunder and lightning? Can God keep the lightning

29

from hurting us? How do we know that God loves us? What can we do if we become afraid in a thunderstorm?

Bible reading for older children and grownups: Psalm 135:5-7.

Let us pray together: Dear Father in heaven, only good things come from You, so lightning must be good for us. Whenever it lightnings, help us to think of how strong You are, and make us happy that we are Your children. We ask this in Jesus' name. Amen.

Beware of coveting. Luke 12:15

Thou Shalt Not Covet

A man once watched a zoo keeper feed a big monkey. The zoo keeper put her food on the floor of the cage. The monkey was all alone in the cage, but she must have been afraid someone else would get part of the food. She grabbed all the food as fast as she could. She stuffed three bananas into her mouth and put an apple under each arm. Then she grabbed a loaf of bread in one hand and a big bunch of carrots in the other.

But there was a big piece of lettuce left on the floor. So the greedy animal put down the carrots, picked up the lettuce, and put it on her head. Then she picked up the carrots again, and went over to a corner of the cage.

The monkey wanted all the food for herself. She was selfish. But she could not enjoy eating it because her mouth was full of the food she was holding. Jesus once said, "Beware of coveting." To covet means to want things selfishly for yourself.

To show how foolish and wrong it is to covet things, Jesus told a story about a rich man who wanted to get richer and richer. He kept on building bigger and bigger barns so that he could keep more and more things in them for himself. But he never thanked God; nor did he help other people. So when the selfish rich man wanted to start enjoying things, God took his life away.

Jesus said, "A person's life does not depend on how much he has." Let's remember this the next time we think we must have certain things in order to be happy. Wanting things often makes people unhappy. The only thing we must have to be happy is the love of Jesus, and we can have that all the time. That's why God's children can be unselfish.

Let's talk about this: How did the monkey show that she was greedy and selfish? Jesus said, "Beware of coveting." When does a person covet? Which story did Jesus tell to show how foolish it is to covet? What is the only thing we need in order to be happy?

Bible reading for older children and grownups: Luke 12:15-21.

Let us pray together: Dear Lord Jesus, please teach us not to covet things, nor to be greedy like a big monkey. Give us those things which we need, and lead us to use Your gifts and blessings for the good of other people. Amen.

31

*Be doers of the word and not
hearers only.* James 1:22

Practicing Your Lessons

Two little girls were playing on the floor. Their mother had company. The people were at the dinner table, ready to start eating. The mother said to the girls, "Please come to the table, girls." But the girls paid no attention to her, not even when she said it two more times.

One of the visitors was the girls' Sunday school teacher. She tried to help the mother. She said to the girls, "I wonder which one of you knows the Bible verse that begins with the words: 'Children, obey . . . .'" Both girls looked up and said real fast, "Children, obey your parents in the Lord, for this is right."

The verse told them to obey their mother, but still they *didn't* obey. What was wrong? The girls were *hearers* of the Word of God, but not *doers*. They knew the words, but they didn't *do* what the words said. Knowing the words didn't help them, did it? Not until they would *do* what they had learned.

To be a child of God and a real Christian, one must do the words from the Bible. The words will not change us and help us until we do what they say. God says, "Be *doers* of the Word and not *hearers* only."

The first thing God wants us to do is to believe in Jesus, our Savior. If we will really do this, we will also want to obey Him in all other ways.

Let's talk about this: What did the mother tell the girls? What did the girls do? How did the teacher try to help? Which Bible words did the girls know? Why didn't the words help them? What is the first thing God wants us all to do?

Bible reading for older children and grownups: James 1:22-25.

Let us pray together: Dear Lord God, we are thankful for Your holy words in the Bible, and we want to hear and learn them. Help us not only to remember them, but also to do what they say. In this way help us to show our love to Jesus, who died for us. In His name we ask this. Amen.

*If God so loved us, we ought also
to love one another.* 1 John 4:11

The Way to Love Everyone

Harold was very nice to people in the store. But at home he was often mean to his little brother. He could be so kind to the people at church, but he was not always kind to his mother.

Sometimes all of us are hard to get along with, especially at home, aren't we? Sometimes we forget. We feel mean. But when we remember how kind and good Jesus was, then we want to be kind and good also. And when we consider that He died to save us, we find it easier to be friendly to other people. Loving Him makes us more like Him.

Jesus said, "Love thy neighbor as thyself." He even told us to love our enemies. He always loved. We often don't.

33

But that's why He paid for our sins on the cross. "If God so loved us, we ought also to love one another."

And don't you think home is a good place to practice loving one another? People could tell what kind of boy Harold really was by the way he acted at home. If we love Jesus, we will want to be kind also to our family in our home.

Let's talk about this: To whom was Harold nice? To whom was he mean? Why ought we to show love especially to the people in our homes? From whom can we learn to be kind? God showed His love to everyone by sending Jesus. How did Jesus pay for our sins? What does our Bible verse say we ought to do because God loved us so much?

Older children and grownups may now read: 1 John 4:10-12.

Let us ask God to help us become more loving: Dear God, we know that You love us even though we are not always lovely, and that You loved everyone in the whole world when You sent Jesus to save all people. Help us to love everybody, and forgive us when we forget. We ask this for Jesus' sake. Amen.

God has made everything beautiful. Eccl. 3:11

Why the World Is So Pretty

Billy and his father were walking along a path near a river. At one spot Billy saw some flowers he had never seen before. "Look how pretty these flowers are," said Billy. "So many colors."

As they walked a little farther, Billy saw some wild strawberries. He picked a few and showed them to his father. "Look how pretty these strawberries are," he said. "They're like a red ice-cream cone on green leaves."

A little later Billy noticed the round stones along the side of the river. They had been washed smooth by the water. He picked some up to take home. "Look how they shine," he said. "Red and yellow and lots of other colors all mixed up."

"Billy," said his father, "I'm glad you can see how beautiful God has made things. Just look at the river and those trees over there and that beautiful blue sky and the green grass all around. The Bible says, 'God has made everything beautiful.'"

"But, Daddy," said Billy, "if God made everything beautiful, why are some things not beautiful any more?"

"That's a good question," said Billy's father. "Some things have been spoiled by sin. People have spoiled things by doing wrong. But God sent His Son Jesus to take away all sin. Jesus came to straighten things out and to make everything beautiful again."

On the way home Billy didn't say much. He was thinking of how good God was in making everything so beautiful.

Let's talk about this: What did Billy notice as he and his father walked along a river one day? Why do you think God made the world beautiful? What do you think is especially beautiful in the world? What was the question that bothered Billy? Why are some things not right and beautiful any more? Who came to take away all sin and to make everything right and beautiful again?

Bible reading for older children and grownups: Matthew 6:28-30.

Let us pray together: Dear Father in heaven, thank You for having made all things beautiful and just right. Forgive us for sometimes spoiling things, and straighten out whatever is wrong with us. Please make our lives beautiful through Jesus Christ, our beautiful Savior. Amen.

*All that is within me, bless His
holy name.* Psalm 103:1

Thank God All You Can

When Jimmy blew his whistle, it was loud and clear. But when he blew it with all his might, it was even louder.

When Jimmy ran, he ran fast. But when he ran as fast as he could, then he really ran fast. Whatever Jimmy did with all his might he really did well.

In Psalm 103 King David told himself that he should thank and praise God. "Bless the Lord, O my soul," he said, "and all that is within me, bless His holy name." He told himself to bless God with everything in him.

If Jimmy were to bless God with everything in him, how would he bless God? He would do it just as well as he could, with everything he's got. That's what David meant when he said, "All that is within me, bless His holy name." He meant to say, "I want to thank God with everything in me."

When somebody gives Jimmy a cookie, Jimmy says, "Thank you." But when somebody gives Jimmy a plateful of ice cream covered with strawberries, he gets excited and says, "Oh, thank you, thank you very much. Thanks a lot!"

Some people thank God a little now and then for things He gives them, but those who remember how He saved them and how He forgives their sins and is good to them every day, they want to thank Him with everything that's in them.

Let's talk about thanking God: When Jimmy blew his whistle as loud as he could, how did it sound? When Jimmy ran with all his might, did he run faster or slower? What did King David tell himself to do? Why did King David want to praise God as much as he could? How will we want to praise and bless God when we appreciate how much He loves us and does for us?

36

Older children and grownups may now read: Psalm 103:1-5.

Let us thank and praise God: If we had a thousand voices, dear God, we would want to use them all in thanking and praising You. Thank You for sending Jesus to die for us. We love You for being kind and good to us instead of punishing us as we deserve. Please forgive us all our sins for Jesus' sake. Amen.

I am your God . . . I will help you. Isaiah 41:10

God's Business

Some children went to a zoo with their mother. There they saw the lions and the elephants and the monkeys and the —

All at once they knew they were lost. They couldn't see their mother anywhere. They didn't know where their car was. They didn't know which way the gate was.

While looking around they saw a sign which said, "IN-FORMATION." Clara went up to the man who sat below the sign. Everybody was asking him questions. Clara didn't really want to bother him, but she had to. She said, "I wish I didn't have to ask you for help, but —"

37

"Oh," said the man, "go ahead and ask. It's my business to help you. That's what I'm here for." He told them which way to go, and soon they found their mother waiting for them by the gate.

Sometimes people think that they shouldn't bother God with all their little troubles. They think that God may have too many other things to do.

What do you think God would say to boys and girls who feel that they shouldn't tell Him about something that bothers them? In the Bible God speaks to us the way the man in the zoo spoke to Clara. God says, "Go ahead and ask for help. I am your God. I will help you."

God wants to help us. He loves to do it. Nothing is too small for Him. Nothing is too big for Him. Big or small, He says, "Don't worry. Don't ever be afraid. I am your God. I will help you."

Let's talk about this: Why didn't Clara want to ask the man for help? What did the man say? In what way is our Father in heaven like the man who helped Clara? How big must a trouble be before we may ask God for help? How big *can* it be? Why is God willing to help us?

Older children and grownups may now read: Psalm 121.

Let us pray together: Thank You, dear God and Father in heaven, for promising to help us at all times. We do not deserve to have You as our God, but we are glad You are. Keep us as Your children for Jesus' sake. Amen.

God said, My love is enough
for you. 2 Corinthians 12:9

Joseph and the Mouse

One day a little mouse came to Joseph. The mouse was very much worried. At first Joseph did not see the mouse, because he was busy figuring how much wheat he had left for feeding all the people. He had mountains of wheat, much more than enough. Then he heard the little mouse squeak.

"What are you worried about, little mouse?" asked Joseph.

"I'm worried that maybe you won't have enough wheat for me," said the mouse.

Joseph laughed, because there was enough wheat to last the mouse a million years or more.

That story was told by Mr. Spurgeon, a great preacher in England. Spurgeon said that one day he was worried about his troubles. He didn't think that everything could come out all right. Then he read the Bible and came to the verse where God says, "My love is enough for you." And then he laughed. He laughed at himself. He was being as foolish as the mouse that came to Joseph and worried that there wasn't enough wheat for it.

Do we ever have troubles? Yes, but not any which God cannot take care of. No matter how much trouble we may have, no matter what we need, God's love can take care of us, and there will always be enough love for us.

So let's remember what God said: "My love is enough for you."

Let's talk about this: What was the little mouse worrying about? Why did Joseph laugh? That story isn't really true, but what does it teach us? Why did Mr. Spurgeon laugh when he read the Bible one day? Is God's love big enough to take care of our troubles? To whom does God give His love?

Older children and grownups may now read: 1 John 5:11-15.

Let us pray: Dear God, we know that Your love is big enough to take care of all our troubles. Forgive us when we do not trust You, and help us to remember that all we need is Your love. Please give us this love for Jesus' sake. Amen.

Be kind to one another. Ephesians 4:32

The Fun of Being Kind

"You didn't make your bed yet, Cliff," scolded his sister Ruth.

"Aw, shut up!" said Cliff. "I'll make it when I want to."

The children were sitting down to breakfast, so their father didn't just pray the table prayer. He prayed, "Please forgive us when we are not kind and friendly, and make us kind to one another, as You are to us. Amen."

"I wasn't kind to Cliff, was I?" said Ruth. "But he wasn't kind to me, either."

"Well, I don't have to be scolded by my sister," said Cliff. "She's not my boss, is she?"

"No, she isn't, and she shouldn't talk like one," said her mother. "But I don't hear her talk that way very often."

"And I haven't heard anyone say 'Shut up!' for a long time in this house," said their father. "I wish I would never hear it again. It isn't very kind."

"Oh, it's awfully hard to be kind all the time when you have brothers," said Ruth, but she was smiling now. Her words were friendly.

"And having some old sisters doesn't help either," grumbled Cliff, who wasn't quite ready to be kind just yet.

"Cliff!" said his mother. But now Cliff smiled, and they all laughed. They were good friends again. Cliff never told Ruth to "shut up" for a whole month. He remembered that God had said, "Be kind to one another." He felt better, too. It was fun being kind.

Let's talk about being kind: Was it wrong for Ruth to tell her brother Cliff to make his bed? Why were Ruth's words unkind? What was unkind about Cliff's answer? What could Ruth have said instead? What could Cliff have said? Which unkind words are sometimes said in our house? Who is happier, the kind person or the unkind person?

Older children and grownups may now read: Ephesians 4:32.

Let us pray to be kind: Please forgive us, dear heavenly Father, our many unkind words. Make us more friendly and kind to people, especially to those in our own home, for Jesus' sake. Amen.

Grieving the Holy Spirit

"Mother, when I sin, am I still a child of God?" asked Mary. She was very much worried.

"What makes you ask?" said her mother.

"Because I made up my mind never to be angry again, but when Buddy splashed mud on my new dress, I got real angry with him. I can't always do only what's right."

"Honey, you have the same trouble I have," said Mary's mother. "I want to obey God all the time, but I find that I don't always, either. Then I must ask for forgiveness and try again."

"But are you God's child even when you sin?" asked Mary.

"Dear, God always forgives us when we are really sorry that we do wrong," said her mother. "Our sins are always forgiven, because Jesus, our Savior, paid for our sins. When you became angry with Buddy, you were still God's child. You always are, as long as you want Jesus for your Savior. But your sin grieved the Holy Spirit. It made Him sad."

"What do you mean, Mother?" asked Mary, a little puzzled.

Mary's mother put her arm around the little girl. "Honey," she said, "God the Holy Spirit lives in the heart of God's children. He lives in your heart. When you sin, He doesn't move out right away. But you make Him sad when you sin. The Apostle Paul tells us, 'Grieve not the Holy Spirit.' That means, don't make Him sad by sinning. Of course, if you keep on making Him sad and you don't want Him to stay, then He may leave."

42

"Oh, I want the Holy Spirit to stay in my heart," said Mary.

First, let's talk about this a little more: About what was Mary worried? Did her mother always do God's will? Why was Mary still a child of God? Why is God always willing to forgive sins? Where does the Holy Spirit want to live? Why do our sins grieve Him or make Him sad? Why will we not want to grieve the Holy Spirit?

Older children and grownups may now read: Ephesians 4:25-30.

Let us pray together: Dear God, please forgive us whenever we get angry or sin in some other way. We love Jesus, our Savior. We want to be Your children. Please keep us from making the Holy Spirit sad, for Jesus' sake. Amen.

The Lord is good . . . and He knows them that trust in Him. Nahum 1:7

God Never Forgets His Children

Jimmy and Betty lived on a farm in North Dakota. One winter day they went home from school in a snowstorm. They couldn't see where they were going. They lost their way. They began to cry for help, but nobody could hear them.

"Nobody knows where we are, so nobody can help us," cried Betty.

"Betty, Somebody *does* know where we are," said Jimmy. "God knows."

"Let's pray for help," said Betty. "Dear Lord Jesus," she prayed, "help us. Please help us."

Soon they heard the bark of their dog near by. He led them to their house, and then they were safe. "God sent the dog," they told their father.

In the days when the prophet Nahum lived, God's people were often afraid of their enemies. But Nahum told them not to be afraid. He said, "Ask God to help you, and depend on Him. The Lord knows them that trust in Him."

Of what are people afraid today? Some are afraid of Communists, some of bombs, some are afraid of not having a job, some are sick and afraid they won't get well. God says to us, "Don't think that I have forgotten My people."

We know that God will not forget us if we are His children and trust in Him. "The Lord is good . . . and He knows them that trust in Him." He will hear our prayers and answer them.

Let's talk about trust in the Lord: Why were God's people afraid in the days of Nahum? What did God tell them? Of whom are people afraid today? What does God tell us? What does "trust in the Lord" mean? Why can we always trust that the Lord will help us? Our Lord Jesus even died for us on a cross. He surely loves us and will answer our prayers. Let's say the Bible verse together.

Older children and grownups may now read: Psalm 91:1, 2, 14-16.

Let us pray for a trusting faith: Dear Lord Jesus, we know that You are good and that You love us. We ought to know enough to trust You always, but sometimes we still become afraid. Please forgive us, and help us to have a trusting faith in You at all times. Amen.

*God will give His angels charge
over you.* Psalm 91:11

Angel Helpers

Long ago, when the prophet Elisha lived, the king of Syria found out that Elisha was telling his secrets to the king of Israel. Elisha knew the secrets because God told them to him. So the king of Syria sent many soldiers to get Elisha.

When Elisha and his helper got up the next morning, his helper became afraid. "Look," he said, "there are enemy soldiers all around the city. They have come for you. What shall we do?"

"Don't worry," said Elisha, "there are more soldiers on our side." Then he asked God to let his helper see the angels around them. All at once his helper saw all kinds of soldiers ready to fight for Elisha. That was how God let the helper see the angels.

Angels are spirits. That is why we can't see them. But they help all of God's children. God sends them to help us, too. What do they do? On some days they may keep things from falling on us and hurting us. On other days they may keep us from getting in front of a fast car or a bus.

We don't know everything that angels do, because we can't see them. But the Bible says, "God will give His angels charge over you." That means, they watch over us if we are God's children. Aren't you glad?

Let's talk about the angels: Why was Elisha's helper afraid? What did God let him see? Did you ever see an angel? Who else in the Bible saw some angels? Can you say the Bible verse? Let us thank God for the angels.

Older children and grownups may now read: 2 Kings 6:8-17.

We pray together: Dear God, our Father in heaven, You give us so many good things which we don't even notice, and we thank You for them. Especially do we thank You today for the good angels who help and guard us. Send them to watch over us every day, for Jesus' sake. Amen.

Be thankful. Colossians 3:15

God Wants Us to Be Thankful

Have you heard about the little children called bloopers? They whine and cry when they can't have their way. Because they're not thankful for good food to eat, they're so skinny and weak, they can just barely squeak. When it's time for a good sleep, they stall and bawl. Something is wrong with them all.

God wants His children to be happy. That's why He tells us to be thankful. When we're thankful, we're happy. People who aren't thankful aren't happy.

Little Karla Jacobs was never satisfied with anything. She didn't like the clothes her mother gave her to wear. She didn't like the food her mother cooked for her. She didn't ever want to do what she was asked to do. Was she happy? Oh, no. She was a very unhappy girl. She was a blooper.

The Bible says, "In everything give thanks." Just think! God loves us. He forgives all our sins for Jesus' sake. We are His children, and someday Jesus will take us to heaven. That is why we can be thankful in everything. And when we are thankful, Jesus is glad, and we are happy.

Let's talk about this: Have we ever been bloopers? When is a person a blooper? Why was Karla Jacobs a very unhappy girl? What does our Bible verse teach us? Why does God want us to be thankful? What are some reasons why we can always be thankful?

Older children and grownups may now read: Colossians 3:15-17.

Let us pray: Dear Father in heaven, we are glad that You always love us and that Jesus died for us on a cross. Help us always to be thankful in everything so that we will be Your happy children and someday be in heaven with You. Amen.

Bless them that curse you. Luke 6:28

How to Treat Mean People

"You are ugly and stupid," said Clara to Ella.

"I guess I am," said Ella, "but in many ways you are very nice."

Clara was surprised. Then she looked up and smiled. "You really aren't ugly and stupid," she said. So now the girls were friends again.

But suppose Ella had become angry and had said mean words back to Clara! There would have been a big quarrel then, don't you think?

Ella wasn't stupid or dumb. She knew how to get around a quarrel and stay friendly. She was bright and sweet.

Jesus told us to do what Ella did. When somebody says mean things to us, we are to say good things back to them. "Bless those who curse you," said Jesus.

God's children are to act that way, because God acts that way. When a man says that he doesn't like God or that he doesn't believe there even is a God, does God keep the rain away from his garden? Oh, no. Does God tell the sun not to shine on his house? Oh, no. God is kind and good even to those who do not love Him. His Son Jesus died on a cross so that everyone could have forgiveness.

So why should we ever refuse to be kind even to those who are mean to us? Jesus wants us to "bless them that curse us." God's children are to be sweet even to those who say hateful things to them.

Let's talk about this: What did Clara say? What did Ella say? Who said the nicest words? How could Ella have gotten even? How does God treat people who don't love

48

Him? What does Jesus want us to do when people hate us and curse us? Who can say the Bible verse?

Older children and grownups may now read: Luke 6:27-31.

Let us pray together: Dear God, You are so good and kind even to those who do not like You. Make us good and kind to everybody. Help us to say nice things even to those who say mean things to us. We ask this in Jesus' name. Amen.

I have sinned. Luke 15:18

The Hardest Words to Say

Only five boys and girls had come to school in the big snowstorm, and now they were guessing riddles.

"A-bra-ca-da-bra is a hard word. Can you say it?" asked Mildred. The other four all tried, but they had it wrong. The answer was "it." (Can you say *it?*)

"I know the hardest words for anybody to say," said Johnny. "I learned them in Sunday school."

"Which words," the others all wanted to know.

"The words 'I have sinned,'" said Johnny.

Do you know what Johnny meant? Is it really hard to say, "I have sinned"?

Suppose you have a quarrel, and someone asks, "Who started it?" Does everybody say, "I did"? Or do they all say somebody else sinned?

Suppose you and your friends played with matches and started a fire. Would everybody say, "I did it," or what would they say?

In a Bible story, a man's son left home with much money

49

and thought he was smart. It took a long time and a lot of trouble before he said, "I have sinned."

But it is good for us to say, "I have sinned." When we say these words to God and mean them, He forgives us for Jesus' sake.

Let's talk about that: Which hard words did Johnny learn at church? Why are those words hard to say? Why is it good for us to say those words to God? For whose sake will our heavenly Father forgive us? How did Jesus pay for our sins?

Older children and grownups may now read: Luke 15:13-18.

Let us confess our sins to God: Dear heavenly Father, we have sinned often, and we have not always acted as Your children today. Please forgive all our sins for Jesus' sake, and help us to be better tomorrow. Amen.

Go away from evil, and do good. Psalm 34:14

How to Keep from Doing Wrong

"Mother," said little Billy, "I wish those bees would go away from me." He meant the bumblebees which were flying close to him. You see, Billy was standing near their nest of honey.

"Then you had better go away from the bees," said his mother. When Billy went away from them, they quit bothering him.

Some people say to God, "I wish my badness would go away from me. I want to be good, but still I do wrong." To them God says, "You had better go away from evil and do good."

Tim and Ella were standing by a fence, looking at the

berries in their neighbor's garden. They knew that it was wrong to pick those berries. But they stood there and looked. The more they looked, the more they wanted those berries. Before long they were taking something that did not belong to them. They were stealing.

What could they have done? They could have walked away and done the dishes which were waiting for them in the sink. Or they could have gone and played with the children next door. Soon they would have forgotten about the berries.

God's children, who love Jesus, are to go away from whatever is wrong. Sometimes walking away helps. And the best way to keep from doing wrong is to love Jesus and to do good. Jesus will help you to do what is good.

Let's talk about this: Why were the bees flying around Billy? What was the only way to get them to quit doing that? What could Tim and Ella have done to keep from stealing berries? What does the Bible verse say we should do? Who will always help us to do what is good?

Older children and grownups may now read: Psalm 34:11-16.

Let us pray to Jesus for help: Dear Jesus, please help us to go away from sin and to do what is good. We know that You had to die on a cross for our sins. Help us to be the kind of children You want us to be, and forgive us when we do wrong. Amen.

*The grass withers, the flower fades, but the Word
of our God will stand forever.* Isaiah 40:8

What the Flowers Said

Irene found the loveliest flowers down by the creek and picked a handful for her mother. When she came home, her mother smiled and put them into a vase. They looked very pretty, but a few of them were drooping already.

The next day Irene looked at the flowers again. They weren't a bit pretty any more. They hung over the edges of the vase. Even the grass that was in with the flowers was drying up.

"Mother," said Irene, "your flowers don't look pretty any more."

"No, they don't," said her mother, "but they teach us a good lesson."

"What kind of lesson?" asked Irene.

Mother put her arm around Irene and said, "The flowers tell us that everything on this earth must die and go away. The pretty flowers die. The grass dies. Do you remember the big dog the neighbors had? It died. And you remember

Mr. Peters who used to build those nice houses. Everything that lives on this earth must die."

"Is that what the flowers say, Mother?" asked Irene.

"Yes," said her mother, "but they remind us of another thing. They say, 'Only the Word of God will never die. Everything that God has said will always be true. It stays the same.' There is a verse in the Bible that tells us this. 'The grass withers, the flower fades, but the Word of our God will stand forever,'" said her mother.

"I'm glad," said Irene. "Whoever believes in Jesus will never die. That's what God has promised."

Let's talk about this: To whom did Irene give some flowers? How did they look at first? How did they look the next day? What always happens to flowers and grass? What will always stay the same? Why was Irene glad that God's promises will never die?

Older children and grownups may now read: Isaiah 40:3-8.

Let us pray: Dear Father in heaven, we enjoy the pretty flowers which You give to us, but we know that they never last very long. Help us to remember that Your Word will last forever. Make us glad to hear and to learn it, and help us to give it to other people so that we and many others will live together with Jesus forever in heaven. We ask this in His name. Amen.

Jesus Christ {is} the same yesterday
and today and forever. Hebrews 13:8

Jesus Never Changes

Dorothy was near to crying. She said, "Yesterday Ethel was so nice to me; and today she acts mean."

"Some people are like that," said her mother. "But are you sure it wasn't *you* who changed? Maybe you were friendly to her yesterday and not very kind today."

"I only told her I didn't like what she said to me," answered Dorothy.

"Well," her mother explained, "most of us change a little every day. On some days we feel real kind, and on some days we are grouchy. It's a good thing God doesn't change like that, isn't it?"

The Bible says, "Jesus is the same yesterday and today and forever." He never changes. He always has loved everybody in the whole world. He still does. And He always will. We can be sure that Jesus loves us every day and never feels mean and unfriendly toward us.

It would be too bad if Jesus were not willing to be good to us on some days, wouldn't it? We would worry if Jesus would change like people often do. But Jesus is always the same. Don't you think we should try to be as much like Him as we can be, always kind and friendly and never any different?

Let's talk about this: What made Dorothy feel like crying? What did her mother tell her? Who doesn't ever change? Why can we be sure that Jesus loves us all day long every day? Let's say the Bible verse together. How does Jesus want us to be all the time?

54

Bible reading for older children and grownups: John 8:46-58.

Let us pray together: Dear Jesus, we are glad that You are always the same loving Savior, always kind and forgiving and helpful. Please make us more like You every day, dear Jesus. Amen.

If a man says, I love God, and hates anyone, he is a liar. 1 John 4:20

Are You a Liar?

"Look, Mother," said Elsie as she showed her mother a card from the Sunday school teacher. It said that Elsie was the best in her class.

"I love God," said Elsie. Then she ran out to play with Wanda in the yard next door.

"Oh, Wanda," she said after a while, "let's go play in your house; here comes that Mexican girl. I don't like her."

So they went into the house. The little Mexican girl had no friends. She saw Wanda and Elsie go into the house. She knew why they went.

The Mexican girl's eyes filled with tears. It hurt to know that people didn't like her just because she was Mexican.

55

Now, if Jesus would write report cards, what do you think He might write on Elsie's? Would He perhaps write, "Elsie is a liar"? God tells us in our Bible verse, "If a man says, 'I love God,' and hates anyone, he is a liar." Elsie knew how much God loved her. Elsie said that she loved God. But she wasn't nice to the little Mexican girl.

Perhaps Elsie did not know that she was hurting somebody. Wanda's mother looked out and said, "That poor Mexican girl. She probably hasn't a single friend to play with. I'm going to give her some of my cookies."

When Elsie saw what Wanda's mother was doing, she remembered how a Christian girl should act. She ran over to Wanda's mother. "May we take the cookies to her?" she asked. When the three girls played together the rest of the day, they were happy.

Let's talk about this: How did Elsie show that she loved God in Sunday school? Was that good? How did Elsie treat the Mexican girl? Who showed Elsie a better way? What does God call people who say they love Him but do not love everybody? What did Jesus do for all people? Is there anyone whom Jesus does not love? Let's say the Bible verse together.

Older children and grownups may now read: 1 John 4:19-21.

Let us ask Jesus for a more loving heart: Dear Jesus, help us to love others as You loved us and all people. Amen.

*Do all things without
murmuring.* Philippians 2:14

The Grumble Box

Over at the Smith home the children were always grumbling. When the potatoes were hot, they grumbled. When the potatoes were cold, they grumbled. They grumbled when they were called to eat, and they grumbled when the dinner was late. The worst of it was, Mr. Smith also grumbled.

One day Mrs. Smith said, "You know, we ought not to grumble all the time. God says, 'Do all things without murmuring.' That means without grumbling or complaining. God wants us to be cheerful people, willing to do whatever is right and good. Here is a box with a slot in the top. Maybe we can learn not to grumble if we will put a penny into the box whenever we grumble. O. K.?"

They all said it was O. K. So the box was put on the middle of the table, and whoever grumbled had to put a penny into the box. By and by they learned to smile and not to grumble. At the end of the month they counted the pennies. There were 213 of them.

Some people grumble wherever they are, not only at home. They grumble at church, they grumble at work; they grumble when it's hot; they grumble when it rains; they just grumble too much.

Maybe we grumble, too. When we must do something we don't like to do, don't we grumble? Are we always cheerful? Perhaps we forget that we are God's children. Are we thankful to God if we complain all the time?

When St. Paul wrote the Bible verse about grumbling, he was talking about doing the things that Jesus wants His

57

people to do. But what he said is true at all times: "Do all things without murmuring."

Let's talk about this: About what did the children grumble in the Smith home? How did Mrs. Smith try to stop them? Was it a good idea? Why do some people grumble wherever they are? About what do we sometimes grumble in our house? What does the Bible verse tell us?

Older children and grownups may now read: Luke 15:25-32.

Let us pray for a cheerful spirit: Dear Lord Jesus, please make us satisfied, cheerful, and thankful, because we have so many reasons to be happy. Keep us from grumbling, because we know that You love us very much. Make us willing and glad to do whatever You want us to do, without grumbling. Amen.

Let us love one another. 1 John 4:7

Do You Love All People?

Mr. Wiser went to church every day. He knew his Bible well. He was nice to people, and people were nice to him.

But to one man he could not be nice. That was Mr. Roberts. Once they had had a quarrel in a meeting. Mr. Roberts had said, "You're a fool." Mr. Wiser never forgot that. He never forgave Mr. Roberts for saying that.

At church Mr. Wiser would not sit near Mr. Roberts. He would not talk to him or look at him. Mr. Wiser hated Mr. Roberts. When you do not like somebody day after day, you are hating him.

One day in church Mr. Wiser heard his pastor preach a sermon about love. "Beloved, let us love one another," the pastor read from the Bible. Then he told how God loved all people. God sent His only Son, Jesus, to die for us and to pay for our sins.

Mr. Wiser began to think. "God is Love," he heard the pastor say. "If God so loved us, we ought also to love one another." Right then and there Mr. Wiser knew that he could not love God if he hated Mr. Roberts. So he asked Jesus to forgive him. From then on he was friendly to Mr. Roberts.

Let's talk about this: How do you feel when you hate somebody? How did God show that He loves everyone? God is Love. He sent Jesus to save all people. If we love Jesus, will we love other people or hate them? If we keep on hating a person, will Jesus stay in our heart? Remember, the Bible says, "Let us love one another."

Older children and grownups may now read: 1 John 4:19-21.

Let us pray together: Dear loving Father in heaven, You are so willing to forgive us and to love us even though we have sinned. Please make us willing to love others for Jesus' sake. Amen.

Jesus said, Come to Me . . . and I will give you rest. Matthew 11:28

Where to Find Rest

Ginny's little rabbit got out of his cage, and a dog chased it. The rabbit went here and there, trying to find a safe place to rest, but the dog kept chasing it. The rabbit was almost too tired to run any more. Just then Ginny stepped out, and

59

the rabbit ran to her. She took the rabbit into her lap and chased the dog away. Now the rabbit had rest.

Sometimes people are just like that rabbit. They are chased by troubles or worries. One boy didn't have any good friends, and he worried about it. Another boy wasn't getting good grades in school, and he cried about this. One little girl had an earache often, and it made her sad. Sometimes our troubles chase us like a dog chases a rabbit.

The world is full of troubles, and the worst trouble is sin. A mother told her little girl not to open the cupboard with the good dishes, but she did anyway. That was a sin. When she broke a dish, she told a lie. "I didn't do it," she said. That was another sin. That night she couldn't sleep because she knew she had done wrong. Sins bring troubles.

To everybody with all his troubles Jesus says, "Come to Me, and I will give you rest." Like the scared rabbit that ran to Ginny's lap, so we can go to Jesus. We go to Him when we pray to Him or when we just think about Him and His love for us.

The little girl prayed to Jesus to take away her sin. Then she went downstairs to her mother and told her she was sorry she had done wrong. After that she felt better and went back to bed and fell asleep. Jesus gave her rest.

Let's talk about this: Where did Ginny's rabbit find rest? Where does Jesus say we can find rest? What kind of troubles do people have? What kind of troubles do we have in our family? What will Jesus do for us? Let's say the verse together and try to remember it.

Older children and grownups may now read: John 14:1-3.

Let us all pray: Thank You for Your promise, dear Jesus, that You will give us rest when we come to You. We know that You forgive all our sins because You love us. That's why we love You. Amen.

Blessed are the peacemakers. Matthew 5:9

The Peacemakers

Bill told Jimmy and Bob, "Come on, we don't want any fights. Let's be friends and play ball." So Jimmy and Bob quit fighting. Bill was a peacemaker.

"Mrs. Jones didn't say any bad things about you," said Mrs. Smith to her neighbor. "She said you were kind."

"Oh, did she?" said the neighbor. "Well, I guess she's a friend after all." Mrs. Smith was a peacemaker.

When the Civil War was over, many people in the North hated the people in the South. Abraham Lincoln didn't. He wanted them all to be friends. Abraham Lincoln was a peacemaker.

All people on earth were disobeying God. God had to punish them. Jesus said, "Let Me take their punishment." So He was punished for us. Now we can have peace with God. Jesus is our great Peacemaker.

"Believe in Jesus as your Savior," said the missionary to the chief of an African tribe. "Ask Him to take away your sins. He will do it." The chief believed that Jesus was his Savior. He believed that Jesus had paid for his sins. Now he had peace with God and was no longer afraid. The missionary was a peacemaker.

The Bible says, "Blessed are the peacemakers."

61

Let's talk about peacemakers: How did Bill make peace? How did Mrs. Smith make peace between her neighbors? Why is Lincoln called a peacemaker? How did Jesus make peace for us with God? How can we be peacemakers?

Older children and grownups may now read: Matthew 5:1-9.

Let us pray: Dear heavenly Father, so many people hate and fight. Help us to make peace wherever we can, especially by telling people about the peace that they can have with You through Jesus, their Savior. In His name we ask this. Amen.

Speak evil of no one. Titus 3:2

Telling the Truth Can Be Wrong

Mr. Jones was a mean man. He always said what he thought, and he told what he knew, even if it hurt other people. He said, "If I think it, I may as well say it. I say what I think. And if it's true, why shouldn't I?" Was he right?

No, he was very wrong. A new family moved to his town. The man had been in jail, but he was sorry for what he had done. He tried to get a job, but Mr. Jones told people, "That man just came from a jail." So nobody wanted the man. Mr. Jones kept the man from getting a job.

It isn't only wrong to tell lies. Sometimes it is wrong to tell the truth, if you tell the truth to hurt someone. God says, "Speak evil of no one." It is always wrong to say something bad about a person, even when it is true, if you are trying to hurt him.

Of course, sometimes we are expected to tell our parents

or teachers the bad things someone else is doing, but Jesus wants us to speak to him first. He wants us to tell bad things about others only when we must in order to help them.

Let's talk about this: What kind of man was Mr. Jones? Did Mr. Jones tell a lie about his new neighbor? Why was it wrong for him to tell the truth? When is it wrong to tell the truth? What does the Bible verse say? Only one Man never hurt anyone by what He said. Who was that? The Bible says that we should be like Him.

Older children and grownups may now read: 1 Peter 2: 21-24.

Let us pray to be kind in what we say: Lord Jesus, we wish we could always be kind and helpful as You are. Please forgive us when we say things that hurt other people. Help us to tell only what is good and what is kind and what is helpful. Please make us more like You. Amen.

Jesus left us an example, that we should follow in His steps. 1 Peter 2:21

Following Jesus

It had been snowing. Mr. Smith walked down the street to the store. On the way he heard a voice behind him.

"Daddy, I'm stepping in your steps!" said his little boy. The little boy was following his daddy and was trying to step right where his daddy's steps were in the snow.

When Mr. Smith noticed what his boy was trying to do, he took smaller steps. When the boy became tired, he carried him the rest of the way.

Little boys and girls like to do what their fathers and

mothers do. We who believe in Jesus are God's children. We want to do what Jesus did. "Jesus left us an example that we should follow in His steps," says the Bible.

But aren't the steps of Jesus too big for us to follow? Yes, they are, if He doesn't help us. But He became a baby and grew up like any other boy. He lived on earth for us and made His steps small so that we could follow them. And then He died on a cross to pay for the wrong steps we take.

When do we follow the steps of Jesus? Well, when Mother wants her girl to help with the dishes, and her girl thinks, "Jesus would do it," and then she does it, too. When Sam wants to let Joe's baseball glove lie in the ditch where he saw it, but he thinks, "Jesus would pick it up," and then he does it, too. Whenever we try to do what Jesus would do, then we are following in the footsteps of Jesus.

Remember, "Jesus gave us an example, that we should follow in His steps."

Let's talk about the example of Jesus, in whose steps we should follow: How can we follow in the steps of Jesus? Do we ever follow Jesus when we do wrong? What are some of the things Jesus did when He was on earth? What are some of the things we can do in order to follow Jesus? Let's say the Bible verse together.

Older children and grownups may now read: John 12:26.

Let us pray: Thank You for Your good example, dear Lord Jesus. Help us all to do what You would do, and forgive us when we don't. Amen.

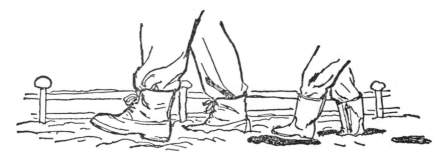

*Thou shalt not . . . bear
any grudge.* Leviticus 19:18

Don't Bear a Grudge

"What is a grudge?" asked the teacher.

"I know," said George. "It's a place where you keep your car." He was thinking of a garage.

But that wasn't what the teacher meant. What she meant was when somebody hurts you and you never smile at him again. When you can't forget a mean thing somebody did to you, then you "bear a grudge."

God says, "You must not bear a grudge."

Nancy came home one day and said, "Mother, I will never talk to Alice again. She said I was dirty." For many days Nancy bore a grudge against Alice. She kept those hurt feelings inside of her. She would not even speak to Alice.

But bearing a grudge is wrong. It is like hating somebody. God does not want us to hate. He wants us to love.

What would happen if God would hate us when we do wrong? What if God would not forgive us? Then we would never get to heaven.

But God loves us. Even though we are sinners, Jesus died for us. If God loved us all that much, we ought to love people, too, even if they aren't always as nice as we want them to be.

Let's talk about grudges: What did George think a grudge was? What is a grudge really? When do people bear grudges? Why is it wrong to bear a grudge? Why does God forgive us everything when we ask Him to do so? Why should we be willing to forgive others? Let's say the Bible verse together.

Older children and grownups may now read: Leviticus 19:16-18.

Let us pray: Dear Lord, You love us enough to forgive our sins every day. Please make us loving, too, so that we will forgive other people, for Jesus' sake. Amen.

I have gone wrong like a lost sheep. Psalm 119:176

When Sheep Get Lost

Farmer Jones had many sheep. When they were eating grass, they behaved very well. But if one of them went wrong, they all wanted to go wrong.

Once one of the sheep saw a hole in the fence. He went through the hole. So did the next sheep, and the next one, until all the sheep had gone through the hole.

Fluffy, a frisky young lamb, went through the hole, too. All of a sudden the neighbor's dog started barking. The sheep became afraid. They tried to find the hole in the fence, but they forgot where it was. They ran all over the field. One sheep broke a leg. One got caught in some bushes and couldn't come home. Fluffy jumped over some tall grass and landed in a mud puddle. She was a very scared little lamb by the time the farmer got her back.

God says that we people go wrong just like sheep. Sheep don't have much sense about going right, and we don't either. We do so many things we shouldn't do. We fight. We tell lies. We are naughty. And we don't do many things God wants us to do. All this is sin.

What can we do about sin? We can tell God about it and ask Him to forgive us and to take us back. We tell God about our sins in the Bible verse for today when we say, "I have gone wrong like a lost sheep."

Let's talk about this: Why does God say that we are like sheep? When do people go wrong like sheep? What are some things we often do wrong? Who is the Good Shepherd who saves us from our sins?

Older children and grownups may now read: Psalm 119:174-176.

Let us pray: Dear God, our Father in heaven, we often are as foolish as sheep. We go wrong and do things You don't want us to do. Please forgive us and bring us back again to where we are safe with You. We ask this in Jesus' name. Amen.

The highway of the upright is to turn away from evil. Proverbs 16:17

The Right Highway

The first time that John tried to drive to a place called Highland he came to a corner. One highway turned right; the other turned left. Which one must he take? He didn't know.

So he walked over to some signs. One sign said, "Highland — 2 miles," and it pointed to the right. Then he knew which highway to take.

Sometimes little children play with cars, and they go on make-believe highways. Let's make believe that our whole

67

life is like a highway. Sometimes we don't know which highway to take.

Jim went to a store. He wished he could buy some candy, but he had no money. The store man was outside, fixing something. Jim could have taken some candy. We might call that highway the "Stealing Street." But Jim turned away from that highway. He did not take the candy. He stayed on "Honest Road."

Selma had a chance to go to a picnic. But her mother got sick and really needed her. "Go ahead to the picnic," said her mother. "But Jesus would want me to help you, Mother," said Selma. So she stayed at home. She didn't take the "Me First" highway. She went on the "Street of Love."

In the Bible God tells us which highway to take. He wants us to take the highway of the upright. The upright are those who do right. And remember, "The highway of the upright is to turn away from evil." To live right, we must also turn away from whatever is wrong.

Let's talk about this: How did John know which highway to take? In which book can we read God's signs? Which highway did Jim choose when he had a chance to take some candy? Which highway did Selma take when she stayed at home to help her mother? Can you think of someone else who took the right highway? What are some highways we will want to take in order to live right? Let's say the Bible verse together.

Bible reading for older children and grownups: Proverbs 16:16-20.

Let us pray: Dear God, help us to understand Your directions in the Bible, and make us willing to follow them. Then we will not go wrong and get lost. When we go wrong, bring us back to the right highway again, for Jesus' sake, because we love Him. Amen.

If anyone will not work, neither should he eat. 2 Thessalonians 3:10

The Right to Eat

A professor had a pile of stones in one corner of his yard. A tramp came to his door one day. "Would you please give a hungry man something to eat?" he begged.

The professor said, "I'll be glad to. If you will move that pile of stones into the other corner of my yard, I'll give you a meal for your work." But the tramp was too lazy to work, so he didn't get to eat.

The professor kept the stones to test the tramps. Every time a beggar came to his house, the professor would say, "I'll be glad to give you a meal. I have a pile of stones I want moved into the other corner of my yard." Those who worked, ate; those who would not work did not get to eat.

Maybe there are better ways to test tramps, but the professor was trying to go by what the Word of God says. "If anyone will not work, neither should he eat," says the Bible.

Every child of God wants to be useful. We will not be useful if we do not learn to work. When a child is very small, he cannot do much. Children have time to play. But they can begin to do little things, like picking up their own toys and helping around the house. By and by they will be able to do more, and someday they will have an important job if they will work hard.

God wants us all to learn to be good workers. Some people are too sick to work, or they just can't get any work. We should be glad to help them. But "if anyone *will* not work, neither should he eat."

Let's talk about work: Why did the professor ask the beggars to move his pile of stones? Can a person be useful

69

and helpful if he doesn't want to work? Why does God want His children to learn to work? Remember, God's children are to be workers. Why do lazy people have no right to eat?

Older children and grownups may now read: 2 Thessalonians 3:7-12.

Let us pray: Dear Father in heaven, we're glad that You want us to be workers, because we want to do things for You. Please make us good workers, who are glad to be useful and helpful. Then we know that You will give us more than enough to eat. We ask this in Jesus' name. Amen.

Out of the heart come
evil thoughts. Matthew 15:19

Where Sins Come From

Jerry had a dream. In his dream he thought that all his sisters and brothers, his father and mother, and all the neighbors could see everything he was thinking. Even when he was thinking something wrong, everybody could see it. So he decided to run away. He didn't think anybody would love him any more.

Jerry was glad when he woke up and knew it was only a dream. It was bad enough to think bad things, but to have people see them would be terrible. He was glad that no one could really see what he was thinking.

Would you like it if people could always see everything you think? All of us think bad things sometimes. All the bad things we do come from our thinking. Why do we say mean words? Because we first think and feel them. Why do we do mean things? Because we think of doing them.

Jesus said that our sins come out of our hearts. "Out of the heart come evil thoughts," He said. And when we think

70

wrong, we do wrong. So let's remember that Jesus wants us to think only good things. He will help us.

Let's think about this some more: Why did Jerry want to run away? Why would you not want everyone to see what you think? How many people are there who never think bad things? Where does our wrong thinking come from? Who washes away our sins and cleans our heart?

Bible reading for older children and grownups: Matthew 15:18-20.

Let us pray for a clean heart: Dear Father in heaven, please take away all the bad and mean things we think about. Make our hearts clean and our thinking right by giving us the Holy Spirit. We ask this for Jesus' sake, who died to save us. Amen.

*A poor man is better than
a liar.* Proverbs 19:22

A Poor Rich Man

The prophet Elisha helped Naaman, a general, to become free of his skin sickness. He told Naaman to wash in the Jordan seven times. When Naaman believed and obeyed, God healed him. Then Naaman came and wanted to give Elisha some gifts. But Elisha did not want Naaman to think that God had helped him get well for money. So Elisha refused to take any gifts from Naaman.

Later Gehazi, Elisha's helper, ran after Naaman. He told the general that Elisha had changed his mind and wanted some money and some clothes for his poor students. So Naaman gave Gehazi much money and two suits of fine clothes. Gehazi hid these in his house.

71

But the prophet Elisha knew what his helper had done. When he came back to Elisha, Elisha said to him, "Where were you, Gehazi?" Gehazi said, "Nowhere." Then Elisha told him, "From now on you will have Naaman's sickness." Suddenly Gehazi's skin became as white as snow. Now he was a leper. It didn't pay for him to lie.

When we tell lies, will we get sick? Perhaps not. God usually does not punish us right away. But lies will not be a blessing to us. God wants us to say only what is true. He does not want us to tell lies, especially not the kind of lies that spoil His work and hurt people.

It would have been better if Gehazi had stayed poor and honest instead of becoming rich and a liar. God says in our Bible verse, "A poor man is better than a liar."

Will everybody who tells a lie go to hell? No, otherwise all people would go to hell. Even good people tell lies sometimes. We are all sinners. But a child of God will want to tell the truth always. And when we have told a lie, God is willing to forgive it for Jesus' sake. Those who love Jesus try hard not to tell a lie the next time.

Remember, a poor man is better than a liar. That means, it is better to be poor than to be a liar.

Let's talk about this: What is so bad about telling lies? Why did Gehazi tell Naaman a lie? How was Gehazi punished by God? How many people in the world have never told a lie? For whose sake is God willing to forgive us? Why will we not want to lie if we love Jesus?

Older children and grownups may now read: 2 Kings 5:20-27.

Let us ask God to make us truthful: Dear Father in heaven, we are glad that everything You have said is true, also Your promises of forgiveness and love. Help us to say only what is true, and keep us from ever lying just to get money or anything else. We pray this in Jesus' name. Amen.

72

*I will sing unto the Lord as long
as I live.* Psalm 104:33

Singing to the Lord

Mamie was feeling blue. So what did she do? She started to sing. "Count your blessings, name them one by one, and it will surprise you what the Lord has done," she sang. So she began to count what the Lord had done for her.

"I have a good home," she said, "while many people lost theirs in the war. I have good clothes — well, anyway, clothes; a cute baby brother, and, oh, so many things. Best of all, I have Jesus as my Friend and Savior, and I know that God loves me."

"Count your blessings, name them one by one," she kept on singing. Soon her sadness was all gone.

Did you ever try singing to the Lord when you didn't feel good? It's better than medicine. It helps you to feel thankful and happy.

Do you ever feel that nobody likes you? Sing "Jesus loves me," and you will feel better. Do you wish you had more friends? Sing "What a Friend we have in Jesus." When you worry about your sins or anything else, sing "I am trusting Thee, Lord Jesus."

While you sit in Sunday school before class or while the organ plays in church, try learning some hymns you don't know. Then when you need them, you will have them in your mind and will be able to sing them. Learn especially those which you like to sing.

People who know and love God say, "I will sing unto the Lord as long as I live." They are happy when they think of how much God loves them.

Let's talk about singing hymns: What did Mamie do when she felt blue? Why does singing a hymn help us to feel better? Which song could we sing if we thought we had no friends? What other hymns do we know? What is the main reason for singing to the Lord as long as we live? Let's say the Bible verse together.

Older children and grownups may now read: Psalm 105:1-5.

Let us pray: Thank You, dear Lord, for Your wonderful love, which comforts us when we are sad and puts a song into our hearts. When we sing our thanks and our joy to You, please accept our prayers for Jesus' sake. Amen.

Teach me Your way, O Lord. Psalm 86:11

Learning God's Way

A little girl was asking her daddy to go along to Sunday school and church. Her mother wished he would, too.

"No, I'm staying home," he said. "You may go if you wish. You go your way, and I'll go my way."

"Daddy, which way are you going?" the little girl asked.

Daddy grunted, but he did not answer. And for a long time he could not forget his little girl's question.

"Which way am I going?" he asked himself. "I'm going the wrong way. I am not going God's way."

74

The Holy Spirit was getting him to think. While his little girl was at church, he tried to read the funnies, but he couldn't. At last he prayed, "Dear God, please help me to go Your way."

Now the man was willing to say what our Bible verse says: "Teach me Your way, O Lord." So he began to read the Bible and to go to church. That's how he found out that God's way to heaven is through believing in Jesus and following Him.

All of us want to go God's way. But how can we know God's way? God teaches us His way in His holy Book, the Bible. The Bible tells us to hate sin and to love our Savior. It also teaches us how to live as a Christian.

God wants to teach us His way when we have devotions. He teaches us in church. He teaches us when we read a Bible story book. And He wants us to study the Bible itself as soon as we can. God's children say, "Teach me Your way, O Lord." And He answers their prayer when they read and study His Word.

Let's talk about God's way: Why didn't the man want to go to church? What did he say? What did his little girl ask? What happened while the little girl was at church? In what book does God tell us His way? How can even a little child learn God's way?

Older children and grownups may now read: Psalm 86:9-12.

Let us ask to go God's way: Dear God, please make us willing to learn Your way, and help us to follow it, for Jesus' sake. Amen.

75

It is more blessed to give than
to receive. Acts 20:35

Giving and Receiving

Jimmy wanted some extra money for a new baseball. So he wrote his mother a note and put it on her plate at lunch time. It said:

Mother owes Jimmy

For running errands	50 cents
For making his bed	10 cents
For picking up his clothes	10 cents
For helping with dishes	15 cents
For practicing piano	15 cents
Total	$1.00

At the supper table Jimmy found a dollar bill on his plate. There was also a note which said:

Jimmy owes Mother

For three good meals a day	Nothing
For washing and ironing his clothes	Nothing
For taking care of him when sick	Nothing
For a good home and lots of love	Nothing
For teaching him	Nothing
Total	Nothing

How do you think Jimmy felt when he read his mother's note? He probably was ashamed of what he had written. The Bible says, "It is more blessed to give than to receive." This means that it is better to give than to get. Giving makes us happier than getting.

Did you ever notice how unhappy children are who always get everything and never learn to give?

The person who gladly shares what he has and tries to help others, he is the happy person. Our Lord Jesus came to give people His love and help. He even gave up His life to save us all. That's why He is such a wonderful Savior. He wants us to be like Him. So try giving instead of getting, and you'll see how much happier you'll be.

Let's talk about this: How did Jimmy try to get some money from his mother? What was she giving to him for nothing? What does the Bible verse say about giving? According to that, who are the happier people, those who give or those who get? What did Jesus give to all people when He died on the cross? Why does giving make us happy?

Bible reading for older children and grownups: Acts 20:32-38.

Let us pray together: Dear heavenly Father, we are glad that You have given us Jesus as our Savior. Help every one of us to be happy by giving instead of trying to get things. For Jesus' sake we ask this. Amen.

God loved us with a great love. Ephesians 2:4

God's Love Is Great

"I don't ever want to see my boy again," said Mr. Johnson, when he heard that the police had caught his son stealing. No matter what his friends said to him, Mr. Johnson would not go to see his boy. And he did not send him any letters either. "My boy might just as well be dead," he said.

One day Mr. Johnson's pastor talked to him. "Jim," he said, "I wonder whether you know how great God's love is. God forgives you all that you do wrong every day, for Jesus' sake."

"I know that God loves me," said Mr. Johnson.

"But if God were like you, it would be harder for Him to love you than for you to love your boy," said the pastor. "Think of how much God has done for you and how often you have disobeyed him. Still He loves you. In the Bible He has said, 'I will never leave you nor forsake you.'"

Mr. Johnson said nothing.

"It may even be that your boy stole because his father was not a good father to him," said the minister very kindly. He didn't want to hurt Mr. Johnson's feelings; he only wanted to show that Mr. Johnson was wrong in not forgiving.

"But even if it was your fault, God still loves you," said the pastor. "'God loved us with a great love,' says the Bible. Even though we were full of sins, He saved us and made us His children. His love in Jesus makes us want to be kind and good."

Mr. Johnson started to cry. Then he promised to go and see his son. God's great love made Mr. Johnson's love bigger.

Let's talk about this: Why didn't Mr. Johnson want to see his boy? Why was this wrong? What did the pastor tell Mr. Johnson? Why does God forgive us even though we do wrong? How did Mr. Johnson show that he forgave his boy?

Bible reading for older children and grownups: Ephesians 2:4-10.

Let us pray: Dear God, we thank You for Your great love. Please forgive us for not always loving people as You do. Help us to have a warm and great love for other people, especially for those in our family. We ask this in Jesus' name. Amen.

You are My friends if you do
what I tell you. John 15:14

How to Be Friends with Jesus

Little Bruce came into the house crying. "Jimmy is not my friend," he said.

"Why isn't Jimmy your friend?" asked his mother.

"Because he won't do what I tell him," said Bruce. Bruce wanted Jimmy to go to the store with him, but Jimmy wouldn't do it.

Most of the time Jimmy did what Bruce wanted, and they were good friends. But when Jimmy did not do what Bruce wanted, or when Bruce did not do what Jimmy wanted, then they were not good friends. The more they did for each other, the better friends they were.

That's how we can become better friends of Jesus — by doing what He wants us to do. He said, "You are My friends, if you do what I tell you."

What is it that Jesus wants us to do? Why, all the things God has said in the Bible — to honor our parents, to help others, to be honest, not to say bad things about other people, and to believe that Jesus is our Savior from sin.

But when Jesus said these words to His friends, He was talking about our loving one another. "Love one another as

79

I have loved you," He said. That's what He meant especially when He said, "You are My friends if you do what I tell you."

Let's talk about this: How can you tell when two people are very good friends? How does Jesus want His friends to treat one another? What will we *not* be if we refuse to do what Jesus tells us? Let's say the Bible verse together.

Older children and grownups may now read: John 15:4-8.

Let us pray: Dear Jesus, we want to be Your friends and Your disciples. Please forgive us for not doing better what You have told us. Help us to do the things that You have told us to do, so that everybody will see that we are Your friends. Amen.

Thy will be done on earth as it is in heaven. Matthew 6:10

Let God Decide

A famous preacher named Moody once took his little daughter Emma to a store to buy her a doll. As soon as they came inside the store, Emma picked out the doll that she wanted. "This is the one I want," said Emma, holding it tightly in her arms. It wasn't nearly as nice as the one her father had meant to get for her, but because her mind was made up, he bought it for her.

The cheap little doll was soon left in a corner. One day Emma's father told her that he had wanted to buy her a much bigger and prettier doll than she had picked out.

"Why didn't you?" she asked. "Because you wouldn't let me," he told her. "Remember?"

Then Emma was sorry she had wanted her own way. After that she always let her father decide what to give her.

80

When he asked her what he should bring her on a trip, she would say, "Whatever you would like me to have, Father." She had learned to trust her father's love for her.

In the prayer which our Lord Jesus taught us to pray, He told us to say to our Father in heaven, "Thy will be done." Our Father in heaven loves us more than Mr. Moody loved his Emma. God even let His Son Jesus die for us so that we could have forgiveness and a home in heaven. He wants us to be His happy and good children. It is better to let Him decide things for us. He always knows what is best.

Let's talk about this: What mistake did Emma make? Why would her father have given her a pretty doll? How did Emma show that she had learned a good lesson? Why did Jesus tell us to say "Thy will be done" to our Father in heaven? Just before Jesus suffered and died for us, He prayed in the Garden of Gethsemane. He said to our Father in heaven, "Not My will, but Thine, be done." What did He mean? Have we learned to say that?

Bible reading for older children and grownups: Luke 22:39-43.

Let us pray: Dear Lord Jesus, thank You very much for letting Your Father's will be done so that we could be saved. Help us to say, "Thy will be done," and to really mean it, so that we will always get what is best for us. We love you. Amen.

As the mountains are round about Jerusalem, so the Lord
is round about His people. Psalm 125:2

God Protects His People

In the days long ago, when they didn't have guns and airplanes, people liked to build their cities on a mountain. There they were more safe from their enemies than on flat ground.

King David built the city of Jerusalem on a hill which had mountains around it. This city was extra safe, because even a few soldiers could stop a big army from coming close. They could fight in the places between the mountains where only a few enemies could get through at a time.

One day David thought of how God is around us like the mountains were around Jerusalem. He thought of how safe God's people are when they trust in Him. "As the mountains are round about Jerusalem, so the Lord is round about His people," he wrote.

But the mountains didn't always save Jerusalem. When the people in Jerusalem became wicked, God let some enemies come and burn up their city. But as long as the people believed and loved God, God protected them.

God can protect us even when mountains cannot. God's children are safe even when airplanes fly over mountains and drop bombs. Nothing can hurt us if we belong to Jesus and stay with Him. God always takes care of His people.

Let's talk about this: How did the mountains help people long ago? Why did King David think that God was like mountains? Why couldn't the mountains keep the people of Jerusalem safe when they were wicked? Why are God's children always safe? Let's memorize the Bible verse. Who can say it from memory?

Bible reading for older children and grownups: Psalm 125.

Let us pray: Dear heavenly Father, with so many dangers around us, we need You like a mountain to protect us. Keep us in Your loving arms. Then we will be safe from all harm and danger. Amen.

I can do all things through Christ,
   who strengthens me. Philippians 4:13

How We Can Be Strong

"I can't do it. I just can't do it," cried Michael as he came into the house.

"What can't you do?" asked his father.

"I can't pick up that big stone in the yard. It won't move. It's too heavy," said Michael.

"Well, now, let's see. Maybe we can move it together," said his father. "I'll help you." So they went out, and with his father's help Michael could move the big stone easily.

There are many things that we cannot do by ourselves. We often say, "I can't do it." But St. Paul said, "I can do all things through Christ, who strengthens me." With Jesus' help we can do anything. How good it is to have Jesus as a Friend and Helper.

Of course, Jesus will not help us with anything that He does not want us to do. But whatever is right and good and pleasing to God He will help us to do. He can make us strong even though we are very weak. All we have to do is ask Him and trust in Him. "Only believe in Me," said Jesus. "All things are possible to him who believes."

Let's talk about this: Why couldn't Michael lift the stone by himself? Who helped Michael do what he couldn't do alone? What are some of the things we cannot do by ourselves? What does the Bible verse say? Why is Jesus able to help us do anything that God wants?

Older children and grownups may read: 2 Corinthians 12:7-10.

Let us pray together: Dear Jesus, our Lord and Savior and Helper, we know that with Your help we can do anything. Help us fight against the devil's temptation, and keep us from sinning. Please help us do whatever our Father in heaven wants us to do, so that we will be strong children of God. Amen.

Underneath are the everlasting
arms. Deuteronomy 33:27

What God's Care Is Like

Long ago Moses wrote, "Underneath are the everlasting arms." What do you think he meant?

Was he thinking of a little boy jumping from a table into his mother's arms? God's care is like a mother's arms.

Was he thinking of a little girl whose father carried her over some water? God's care is like a father's arms.

Was he thinking of an eagle? The mother eagle flies under her young eagles when they are learning to fly. When they fall, the mother eagle catches them on her back and flies them safely back to their nest.

The everlasting arms under us are God's arms. This is picture talk. We cannot see God's arms. But God tells us that nothing bad can happen to His children because "underneath are the everlasting arms."

God's arms are everlasting; they never get tired; they are never too weak to help us; they are always under us.

Let's talk about this: Does it happen very often that a father drops his child? Could it happen? Why don't God's arms ever get tired and weak? Are you willing to let God take care of you in everything? Let us remember that God's arms are always under us.

Older children and grownups may now read: Psalm 46:1-3.

Let us thank God for His love and care: Dear heavenly Father, we are thankful that Your arms are under and around Your children at all times. Hold us close to You, and when we fall into sin or any other trouble, reach out and save us, for Jesus' sake. Amen.

Jesus said, I am the Way. John 14:6

The Escalator to Heaven

Sandra always liked to go with her mother to the big store in the big city. She would stand on the bottom step, and the escalator would take her up to the next floor. "I like to ride the escalator," said Sandra to her little brother Jimmy.

"What's an escalator?" Jimmy asked her.

"It's steps that move. You don't walk up; they carry you up," said Sandra.

"Oh," said Jimmy. "Jesus is like an escalator. He takes people up to heaven." Jimmy had a pretty good idea.

85

Long ago the disciple Thomas asked Jesus, "How can we know the way to heaven?" Jesus didn't say, "I'll show you the way." He said, "I *am* the Way." He doesn't just *show* people how to get to heaven; He *takes* them there Himself.

So you see, in a way Jesus is like an escalator. Those who know Jesus and love Him and trust in Him are on the way to heaven. Jesus said, "I am the Way." If you will stay with Jesus, He will take you up to heaven.

Lets' talk about this: What is an escalator? Why did Jimmy call Jesus an escalator? What did the disciple Thomas once ask Jesus? What did Jesus answer? What must we do to get to heaven? When will we get there if we stay with Jesus?

Older children and grownups may now read: John 14:1-6.

Let us bow in prayer: Dear Jesus, we are glad that You are the Way to heaven. We know that we cannot get there by ourselves, and we want You to take us there. Please keep us close to You every day so that we will always be on the Way. We ask this because we know that You are our Lord and Savior. Amen.

God has put gladness in my heart. Psalm 4:7

When You're Happy Inside

"When Mrs. Jacob smiles, I don't think she means it," said Jane. "She just smiles a little bit with her mouth and then stops."

"It's hard to smile on the outside when you don't smile on the inside, too, isn't it?" said her mother.

"Yes," said Jane, "so I thought I would bring Mrs. Jacob a flower. Maybe then she will be glad inside, and her smile will look better."

"That's a good idea," said her mother. "And you reminded me of a little Bible verse which tells how to get happy on the inside."

"Tell me," said Jane.

"It's something King David said in a psalm he wrote. 'God has put gladness in my heart,' he said."

"What made King David say that, Mother?" asked Jane.

"Well," her mother answered. "Let's see." Then she went and looked in her Bible at Psalm 4. "First he said to God, 'Have mercy on me, and hear my prayer.' Then he said to himself, 'The Lord will hear when I call to Him.' So I guess God made him happy by promising to love and help him."

"God loves us, too," said Jane.

"You know He does," said her mother. "He even let His Son Jesus die for us on a cross. Jesus died to pay for our sins, and now God forgives us and smiles at us."

"If God is smiling at us, He really means it, doesn't He?" said Jane.

"Yes," said her mother. "And when we know that He loves us, it makes us glad inside; and then we can smile real easy on the outside, too."

Let's think about this: What bothered Jane? Why was it hard for Mrs. Jacob to smile on the outside? What had made King David happy in his heart? How do you know that God loves you? How do you feel on the inside when you believe that God is smiling at you? When you're happy on the inside, how will you be able to smile on the outside?

Bible reading for older children and grownups: Psalm 4.

Let us pray: You have put gladness in our hearts, dear God. Please help us to remember that You love us, so that we will always be happy on the inside. Then it will be easy to smile on the outside and really mean it. We ask this in Jesus' name. Amen.

Jesus prayed, Father, forgive them, for they know not what they do. Luke 23:34

What We Do When We Sin

Len was playing ball in his back yard. He stepped on some flowers his mother had just planted. "I didn't know I was doing it," said Len to his mother when she called to him. His mother saw that Len didn't know he was standing on her flowers, so she forgave him.

When Jesus was ready to die for us, some soldiers took Him and nailed Him to a cross. They had to do it; their officer told them to do it. But they didn't know that it was their Savior they were nailing on the cross. They did not know that Jesus was their Lord and God.

So Jesus prayed for them as they pounded nails into His hands and feet. "Father, forgive them," He said, "because they do not know what they are doing." Jesus loved even the men who were hurting Him.

When we do wrong, let us remember that we are hurting Jesus more than the nails hurt Him. When we are mean and nasty or tell a lie or disobey our parents or steal, let's not forget that Jesus had to die for those sins, too.

But Jesus also prays for us. He still says, "Father, forgive them, because they do not know what they are doing." If we will think about what we are doing when we sin, it will help us to keep from sinning.

Let's talk about this: What did the soldiers do to Jesus? How did Jesus pray for them? Whenever we do wrong, we hurt Jesus, too. Why did Jesus let the soldiers nail Him to a cross? What does Jesus want His Father to do for us? If we love Jesus, what will we not want to do?

Older children and grownups may now read: Luke 23:33-43.

Let us thank Jesus for His great love: Dear Jesus, You were so kind when the soldiers were hurting You. Please ask Your Father to forgive our sins, too. Help us to remember that also our sins hurt You. And keep us from doing wrong, because we love You. Amen.

God loves a cheerful giver. 2 Corinthians 9:7

Do You Like to Give Things?

"Mother, I don't want to give Emma anything for her birthday this year," said Myra. "She never gives me anything."

"She hardly can," said Myra's mother. "Her parents are very poor. But do you give presents so you can get some back?"

"Well — I guess so," said Myra, feeling a little ashamed.

"Look, Honey," said Myra's mother, putting her arm around her. "You'll never be happy if you give to get. Do you know what the Bible says about giving?"

"What?" asked Myra.

"It says, 'God's children should give what they want to in their heart. They are not to give when they don't want to or because they think they have to. God loves a *cheerful* giver.'"

"You mean, God wants us to be happy when we give things to other people?" asked Myra.

"Yes," said her mother, "because He gave us His Son Jesus as a gift, and He gives us His love and anything we need."

"Jesus wants us to give to poor people, doesn't He?" said Myra.

"Yes," said her mother, "and that's one way of showing our love to Jesus."

"Mother," said Myra, "will you let me take a big cake to Emma for her birthday? She never has a birthday cake."

Myra's mother gave her a big hug. "God loves a cheerful giver," she said again.

And the next day, when Myra took the cake over to Emma, Emma was so happy. She also hugged Myra. When Myra came home, she said to her mother, "It was fun doing what pleases Jesus."

Let's think this over: Why didn't Myra want to give Emma a present? What did her mother tell her? What kind of giver does God love? What special reason do we have for giving cheerfully to others? Why did Myra's mother hug her? Why did Emma hug her?

Older children and grownups may now read: 2 Corinthians 9:6-8.

Let us pray: Dear Lord Jesus, please keep us from being selfish with what we have. Help us to be thankful that You gave us Your life and everything we have. Make us willing to show our thanks by being cheerful givers especially to those who need help. Amen.

I enjoy doing Your will,
   O My God. Psalm 40:8

A Good Way to Have Fun

A rich man was feeling sad. He thought he was sick, so he went to a doctor. The doctor guessed what was really wrong. So he said, "Take $5,000 and visit poor people this week. Buy them what you think they need, and help them if you can."

The rich man did this. The next week he came back to the doctor and said, "I never had so much fun in my life. It was the best medicine I could have taken." He was right. You will enjoy doing good and helping the poor and needy.

Some people think that Jesus was always sad, but most of the time He was very happy. He enjoyed helping people. He enjoyed being with people at weddings and dinners. He enjoyed teaching them God's Word. He even was glad to suffer and die for all of us. He did all this in order to save people from their sins.

Long before Jesus became a man on earth, He said, "I enjoy doing Your will, O My God." He loved to do whatever the heavenly Father wanted Him to do. He enjoyed doing God's work.

Can you say, "I enjoy doing whatever You want me to do, O my God?" Are you glad to do God's will? If you love Jesus and want to be like Him, you will enjoy doing whatever God wants you to do.

Let's talk about this: What do you think was the matter with the rich man? How did he forget his troubles and become happy? Was Jesus happy in helping people? What else was Jesus glad to do for all of us? Why did Jesus enjoy doing whatever our Father in heaven wanted Him to do? Will we gladly obey God if we love Him?

91

Older children and grownups may now read: Psalm 40:1-3, 7, 8.

Let us pray together: Dear Father in heaven, we want to enjoy doing Your will as Jesus did when He lived on earth. Often we do not obey You, but please forgive us for Jesus' sake. Help us to love You more so that we will enjoy doing whatever You want us to do. Amen.

Ho, everyone who thirsts, come to the water, and he that has no money, come! Buy and eat! Isaiah 55:1

God's Gifts Are Free

Imagine a little boy standing across from a big grocery store. In front of the store are heaps of apples and oranges and other fruit on a stand. Inside are bread and milk and lots of other food. But the little boy hasn't eaten all day because he has no money and his parents are both at work.

Then the man who sells all those good things comes out of the store and waves to the boy and others passing by. The boy hears him say, "Hey, everyone who is thirsty, come and get a free drink; and if you have no money, come anyway and buy and eat!"

The boy can't believe it, but he is thirsty and hungry, and it sounds good. So he runs over and says that he would like some milk. "I have no money," he says, but the man gladly gives him all the milk he wants. Then the boy points bashfullike to some bananas, and the man sticks three big ones in the boy's pocket. When the boy starts to leave, the man also gives him a whole loaf of bread, a box of cookies, a quart of ice cream, and all the apples he can carry.

That isn't what most storekeepers would do. But it is

92

what God does. One day God's prophet Isaiah said, "Ho, everyone who is thirsty, come to the waters, and he that has no money, come, buy and eat." He was thinking of the good things God has for us and how we can have these good things without paying for them. In the Bible God invites everybody to come and enjoy His gifts without paying for them.

Do you know what the water and bread is that God wants us to buy from Him without money? His love and the forgiveness of all our sins. For Jesus' sake God wants to give us His love free for nothing. All we need to do is believe what He has told us in the Bible. It's almost too good to believe, isn't it?

Let's think about this: How do you think the hungry boy felt when he was given free food? What is the bread and water that God wants us to have? How much do we have to pay for God's love? Who all may have God's love and blessings? How can anyone get God's gifts without paying anything for them?

Bible reading for older children and adults: Isaiah 55:1-3.

Let us pray together: Dear Father in heaven, how glad we are that You are willing to give Your love to everyone free of charge. Help us to believe Your Word so that we will take Your gifts and have life with You forever. We ask this in the name of Jesus, our Savior. Amen.

He that is slow to anger is better
than the mighty. Proverbs 16:32

The Better Way

Mrs. Jones came rushing up to the door. She hardly gave Mrs. White time to open it before she started to scold. She was from the big house with the wide lawn across the street.

"I'll have you know that I don't want your children to run over my lawn and flowers," said Mrs. Jones even before she sat down. "I knew when you moved in that you weren't much good. We try to keep our lawn looking neat, but when people move in who don't care how things look, that's just too bad."

"When did this happen?" asked Mrs. White.

"Don't act so innocent," said Mrs. Jones. "You know well enough it happened yesterday afternoon. You probably told them to do it."

"But the children and I weren't at home all day yesterday," said Mrs. White. "We went to my mother's house early in the morning, and we came back after dark."

"Oh," said Mrs. Jones and got up. She left without saying another word.

After that, Mrs. White started to cry. But Mr. White came into the room and said, "Don't cry, Mother. Mrs. Jones may be rich and important, but I'd much rather have a gentle wife like you than an angry and proud woman like Mrs. Jones. You acted the way Jesus would want you to act."

The next morning there was a letter in the mail from Mrs. Jones, saying that she was sorry. The Bible says, "He that is slow to anger is better than the mighty."

Let's talk about anger: Why was Mrs. Jones angry? Why didn't Mrs. White get angry? What might have happened if Mrs. White had gotten angry, too? What makes it hard to keep from getting angry and hateful? Which is better, to act big and tough or to be kind and gentle? Why? Let's say the Bible verse together.

Older children and grownups may now read: Proverbs 16:27-30.

Here is a little poem to remember:

> Christ is kind and gentle;
> Christ is pure and true;
> And His own dear children
> Must be holy, too.

This is My commandment, that you love one another as I have loved you. John 15:12

Something Jesus Wants Very Much

"I told you twice to pick up your clothes," said a mother to her boy Tommy. She shouldn't have to tell him twice, should she?

There's something Jesus told His disciples twice in a row. He must really want us to do it. "Love one another," He said twice at one time, and in between He said, "You are My friends if you do what I tell you."

Why did Jesus say "Love one another" two times in a row? Perhaps because every once in a while Peter was angry with Philip, and Nathanael quarreled with Thomas, and the others often were jealous. They needed to be told twice.

Boys and girls often quarrel in their home or at school. They get angry very easily, they say bad words to each other, and some even hit and pull hair and do other mean things.

95

Do you know what Jesus wants them to do? He said, "This is My commandment, that you love one another as I have loved you."

How much did He love us? So much that He died for us on a cross. That much we are to love one another. That's quite a lot, isn't it? Would you be willing to die for someone else? Jesus died for all people. He died to save them from their sins. He wants us to love the way He loved us.

Let's talk about this: What is the commandment Jesus gave to His disciples? Why do you think Jesus said these words twice? Who needs to remember that God wants His children to love one another? How much should we love one another? How much has Jesus loved all of us?

Older children and grownups may now read: John 15:12-17.

Let us pray: Dear Lord Jesus, we are sorry that we have not loved one another as much as we ought to. Please forgive us, and help us to have such a love as Yours. Then we will love one another as You have loved us, and that will be wonderful. Amen.

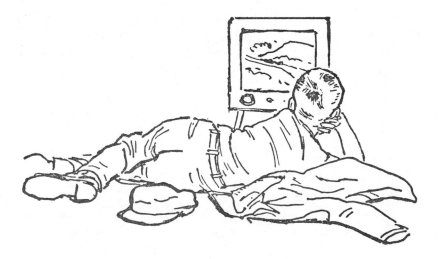

Jesus said, Don't be afraid,
  only believe. Mark 5:36

Never Be Afraid

When the man left his little girl, she was very, very sick. So he went to Jesus and begged Him to help her. On the way to his house somebody came and told the father, "Your little girl is dead. Don't bother Jesus any more."

Jesus heard what was said. He saw the father get white in the face. The father thought Jesus could not help him now. So Jesus put His hand on the man's shoulder and said, "Don't be afraid; only believe. I can still help you."

Together they went to his home, and Jesus made the girl alive again. She wasn't even sick any more.

Jesus can help when nobody else can. Jesus can help even when nobody thinks He can. But we are to believe in Him and trust Him and we must want His help.

So if ever we are in trouble, let's not forget Jesus. He loves all people just as much today as He did when He was on earth, and He is just as strong. If we will believe that He can help us and wants to help us, we won't ever be afraid. And we will find out that He always helps in one way or another.

Let's talk about this: What did the father ask Jesus to do? What did a man come and tell the father? Why did the father become afraid? What did Jesus say? What did Jesus do? Why can Jesus help us in any kind of trouble? Why need we never be afraid when we believe in Jesus? Let's say the little Bible verse together.

Older children and grownups may now read: Mark 5:35-43.

97

Let us pray: Dear Jesus, we believe that You are the Son of God and our loving Savior. Please help us to believe in You so that we will always trust You. Then we won't be afraid even to die, because You give people a life that never ends. Amen.

As the heaven is high above the earth, so great is
  His mercy toward them that fear Him. Psalm 103:11

The Greatness of God's Love

Once a farmer's little boy asked his father, "How big is the sun?" The farmer answered, "Oh, maybe about as big as a load of hay."

"That's awfully big," said the boy; "it doesn't look that big."

But really the sun is much bigger than a load of hay. It is bigger than the whole earth on which we live, much bigger. We just can't see how big it really is. We can't even imagine how big it is.

How big is the love of God? It, too, is much bigger than we think. As high as the heaven is above the earth, higher than anybody could climb or fly or see, so great is God's mercy toward them that fear Him, says the Bible. If God's love were like a tree growing straight up, nobody could ever find the end of it, because God's love doesn't have any end.

God's mercy is toward them that fear Him. Who are the people that fear God? Not those who are afraid of God, but those who love Him and are afraid to sin. Those who love God so much that they don't ever want to sin, they fear God in the right way. And those who fear God and are sorry for their sins will find that God's love is very great, always big enough to forgive them.

98

Let's think about this: How big did the farmer say the sun was? How big is the sun really? How big does the psalm say God's love is? Whom does God love in a great big way? Who are the people that fear God in a right way? What are some of the sins we will be afraid to do if we really love God? What does God always do for Jesus' sake as long as we are sorry for our sins?

Bible reading for older children and adults: Psalm 103:8-13.

Let us thank God for His great love: How wonderful is Your love, dear God, and how great! Help us to fear You in the right way, to love You so much that we will never want to sin. When we do sin, please forgive us for Jesus' sake. Amen.

A friend loves at all times. Proverbs 17:17

How to Have Good Friends

"I hate Helen. She said my hat looks funny," grumbled Mary, with her lower lip stuck 'way out.

Dan, her big brother, looked at her. "I thought Helen was your friend," he said.

"She's not my friend if she says mean things to me," said Mary.

"Maybe you're not a good friend either if you get angry at your friend," said Dan. "Do you remember the Bible verse you learned about a friend?" he asked.

"Which one?" asked Mary.

"You know — the one that says, 'A friend loves at all times.'"

Mary remembered. She had learned it in Sunday school. "Oh, sure," she said. "A friend loves at all times."

"When Helen said your hat looked funny, you could have said, 'Does it? What makes you think so?' Then maybe you'd still be good friends," Dan told his sister.

"I guess I'm the one who wasn't a good friend, 'cause I stopped loving Helen," Mary admitted.

"Now you're on the right track," said Dan. "It's a poor friend who gets angry easily. A real friend loves at all times. Just think of how Jesus loves us at all times. That's why He's called the best Friend anyone ever had."

"You know what, Dan?" said Mary, grinning, "I don't hate Helen any more. I want to keep on being her friend."

Let's talk about friends: Why did Mary say she hated Helen? Which Bible verse did her brother Dan tell her? Why wasn't Mary being a good friend to Helen? Who is the best Friend anyone ever had? What is Jesus willing to do for us at all times?

Bible reading for older children and grownups: Proverbs 17:13-17.

Let us pray together: Dear Father in heaven, please help us to be really good friends who don't quit being friends over little things. Help us to be the kind of friends Jesus always is to us. We ask this as His children. Amen.

I am ... wonderfully made. Psalm 139:14

Your Wonderful Body

Bobby cut his finger on a tin can. He came running into the house. His mother had him hold his finger under the faucet while she looked for a bandage.

"Why does the finger bleed?" asked Bobby.

"Because God wants the blood to wash the place where you cut yourself," said his mother. "The can was dirty. We will clean the cut with medicine, but the blood washes it, too."

After a while Bobby said, "It stopped bleeding now."

"Fine," said his mother. "Now the blood will cover the cut. Then new skin will start to grow under the dry blood."

"God makes the blood work that way, doesn't He?" said Bobby.

"Yes," said his mother. "The Bible says, 'The Lord made us.' In another place it says, 'I am wonderfully made.'"

"You know what else is wonderful?" asked Bobby. "Fingernails! When my nail came off last year, it hurt to grab things. Now I have a new fingernail."

"That's right," said his mother. "And your eyes are wonderful, and your hands, and your tongue, and your toes."

"That's 'cause God made me," said Bobby.

Let's talk about this: Can you think of anything that is more wonderfully made than you are? Who made you? What wonderful things have you noticed about your body? If a man loses a hand, what kind of hand can he get? Will it be as good as the one God gave you? Because God made you, to whom do you belong? What are some ways of thanking God for your body and for His love?

Older children and grownups may now read: Psalm 139:1-14.

Let us thank God for the way He made us: Thank You, dear heavenly Father, for having made us so wonderfully well. Help us to take care of our bodies, and teach us to please You in whatever we do, for Jesus' sake. Amen.

The Lord has done great things for us,
and we are glad. Psalm 126:3

Why Christians Are Glad

"Oh, boy, isn't this a nice home!" said Dan. Their old house had burned down, and they were moving into a new one. He ran upstairs to put the first piece of furniture into his room — he had a room all his own now. His brothers and sisters were just as happy as he, and his father and mother were, too.

That night, when everything was unloaded, just before it was time to eat, Dan's father said, "Now let's all sit down in the living room and thank God for doing so much for us. He took care of us when our old house burned down; and now He's even giving us a better one than we had."

Everybody dropped what he was doing and came into the living room. But before saying a prayer of thanks, Dan's father read a psalm — Psalm 126. It's a poem in which God is praised for letting His people return to their country after some enemies had taken them away.

Then the mother said, "I think we should all remember a verse from that psalm. It will help us to stay thankful for what God has done for us."

"I know which verse you mean," said Dan. "'The Lord has done great things for us, and we are glad.' It's true, too."

They all said the verse together, and Dan's father led them in prayer. "Thank You, dear Lord, for having died for us, for having made us God's children, for watching over us, for blessing us with a new home," he said. "Help us to be thankful always. Amen."

Let's talk about this: Why was Dan happy? What had happened to Dan's old house? When everything was unloaded what did Dan's father want to do? Which psalm did he read? Which verse did Dan's mother want them all to remember? What great things has the Lord done for all of us? Has He done anything special for our family?

Older children and grownups may now read: Psalm 126.

Let us thank the Lord together: Dear Lord Jesus, You have done so many great and good things for us, and we are glad that we are Your children. Help us to show our thanks in all that we do, and please keep us in Your love. Amen.

*Whoever will be chief among you, let him
be your servant.* Matthew 20:27

How to Become Great

Mr. Black could hear the children quarrel in the back
yard. Each one was shouting "First," and nobody wanted
to be second. So he took some popcorn out to them. While
they were eating and being quiet, he told them this Bible
story:

The helpers of Jesus, the twelve disciples, started quarreling one day. Every one of them thought he should be
the chief. When Jesus heard about this, He called His friends
together and said, "Some people try to rule other people,
but you must not be that way. Whoever wants to be chief
among you, let him be your servant." That meant, if you
want to become a great Christian, you must do things for
others.

Jesus said, "I didn't come to be served, but to serve, and
to give My life for other people." Jesus wants His friends
and helpers to be like Him.

Then Mr. Black said, "Now tell me, who do you think
is the best player: the one who always wants to bat or pitch,
or the one who will play where he can help the team most?"
They all said, "The one who will play where he can help
the most."

"It's like that in everything else, too," said Mr. Black.
"If we want to be really important, we can't get that way by
being bossy. We must try to be helpful, giving up things for
other people. Remember, Jesus even gave up His life for us."

Let's think this over: Why were some children quarreling? Which Bible story did Mr. Black tell them? What
kind of ballplayer is the best kind of player? How are the
104

friends of Jesus to become great? What did Jesus give up in order to help all people?

Older children and grownups may now read: Matthew 20:20-28.

Let us pray together: Dear Lord Jesus, forgive us when we try to be important by pushing other people around. Help us to remember that You want us to become great by doing things for other people. We are thankful that You were willing to die for us, and we love You for it. Amen.

Let another man praise you, and not
  your own mouth. Proverbs 27:2

Don't Blow Your Own Horn

Jesus once told a story to people who thought they were better than others. It is called the story of the Pharisee and the Publican. The Pharisee prayed something like this: "I thank You, God, that I am better than other people, better than cheaters, better than unfair people, or people who aren't decent. I do more good things than I have to. I often go without eating. And I give God ten cents out of every dollar I get."

That was what the man said. But God did not like his prayer. It wasn't really a prayer at all. He was just telling God what a good man he was. He was praising himself. He was bragging.

God doesn't want a person to say how good he is. "Let another man praise you, and not your own mouth," says the Bible. When we praise ourselves, we are proud. God would rather have us ask Him for forgiveness of sins and for help in becoming better.

105

But when other people praise us, it's all right; and they will, if we really do good things. They'll notice what we do without our telling them. And even if they don't, Jesus will.

Remember, it's better to have Jesus and other people praise you than to praise yourself.

Let's talk about this: How did the man pray who thought he was good? Why wasn't this a prayer? What would Jesus rather have us say in our prayers? Why doesn't God want a person to praise himself? Who will praise us when we do good?

Older children and grownups may now read: Luke 18:9-14.

Let us pray: Dear Father in heaven, we know we are sinners. We are far from being what we ought to be. Please forgive our sins and make us more like Jesus so that someday You will be able to praise us. We ask this in Jesus' name. Amen.

The Lord knows them that are His. 2 Timothy 2:19

God Can See Who Believes

Everybody in Hope Church was talking. Older people were shaking their heads. The president of the church had cheated by not paying enough taxes. He had to go to jail for that.

"He was a bad man, wasn't he?" said Ray.

"Let's say he was a sinner," said Ray's father. "We are all sinners."

"But he can't go to heaven if he cheated, can he?" asked Ray.

106

"Can a boy who hits his sister expect to be in heaven?" asked his father. Ray hung his head. He had hit his sister that morning.

Then Ray remembered and looked up. "If he is sorry for what he does wrong and asks Jesus to forgive him," said Ray, "then he can."

"Can what?" asked his father.

"He can go to heaven," said Ray. "God forgives all sins for Jesus' sake when we ask Him. Isn't that so?" asked Ray.

Ray's father was surprised that he knew so well the things he had learned about God. "Yes," he said, "God so loved the world that He gave us His only Son, Jesus, to be our Savior. Whoever believes in Him will not die, but will live with God in heaven always. Maybe the man who went to jail asked God to forgive him."

"But how do we know who believes in Jesus?" asked Ray. "Maybe some people just say they do."

"I hope not," said his father, "but God knows. The Bible says, 'The Lord knows them that are His.' He knows whether you want Jesus to be your Savior. You can't fool Him."

Let's talk about this: Why did the president of Hope Church have to go to jail? How could he still get to heaven? What showed that Ray was a sinner too? For how many people did Jesus die on the cross? Why? Who all receives forgiveness of sins from God? Who knows whether a person really believes in Jesus? Let's say the Bible verse together.

Bible reading for older children and adults: 2 Timothy 2:15-19.

Let us pray: Dear Lord, we want to belong to You. Please keep us from sin, and when we sin, please forgive us. Help us always to believe that You died on a cross for all sinners, including ourselves. Please let us all be in heaven with You someday through Your love. Amen.

My little children, let us not love in word, neither in tongue,
but in deed and in truth. 1 John 3:18

Talk Is Cheap

"I love you, Mother," said little Nell; "I love you more than my tongue can tell." Soon after that Nell went out to play and left her mother alone with the dishes — dishes Nell could have done for her mother.

"I love my dad," said Bob. But when he heard his dad cutting the lawn, he hid in the basement until the job was done. He was afraid he might have to help.

"I love Jesus," some people say. But then they aren't willing to be like Him. He gave His life for people and wants us to love one another as He loved us.

You may say, "I love all other people." But if you have something someone else needs and you refuse to give it to him, do you really love that person? Or if you can help a

108

person who needs help and you don't, are you loving the way God loves?

It's easy to say, "I love you," isn't it? It's easy to say, "I love Jesus." But the one who really loves shows his love not only by what he says but also by what he *does*. St. John said, "My little children, let us not love in word, neither in tongue, but in deed and in truth." Words aren't true unless they are proved by deeds.

Now let's talk about this: What did Nell say to her mother? What did she do? What did Bob say? What did he do? How are we to show that we love Jesus? What would show that we do not love some other person even when we say we do? Let's learn the Bible verse by saying it together several times.

Bible reading for older children and grownups: 1 John 3:16-18.

Let us pray: Dear Lord, forgive us for not always loving people by helping them. Help us to really love You and people by what we do and not just by what we say. Amen.

Say not, I will do to him as he has done to me. Proverbs 24:29

Take No Revenge

"When I get him, I'll give him *two* black eyes," said Ralph.

"Why, what happened?" his father asked.

"Roy hit me in the eye with his elbow."

"I'm sorry you got hit," said the father, "but Roy probably didn't mean for his elbow to get into your eye."

"It hurts just the same," said Ralph.

"It probably does," said his father. "So now you want to give Roy *two* black eyes. If you would, what do you think he'd want to do to you?"

"Probably hurt me worse," said Ralph.

"And so it could keep on. Each time somebody would hurt the other one worse than before. Do you think it would be a good idea to let that go on for a month?"

"No, I guess not," said Ralph.

"How, then, can you stop it from going on?" his father asked.

"Well, I guess I just won't hit him at all," said Ralph. And that was a much better plan than Ralph had had at first.

The Bible tells us, "Say not, I will do to him as he has done to me." Jesus prayed even for those who nailed Him to the cross. He said, "Father, forgive them." He forgives all of us our wrongs.

Of course, a Christian may defend himself, but he is not to try to get even. God's children ought never to say, "I will do to him as he has done to me." God's children ought to be like Jesus, their Savior. He never tried to get even.

Let's talk about revenge: Why was Ralph angry? What might have happened if Ralph had hurt Roy in return? When we hit someone back because he has hit us, does that make things better or worse? What is the difference between defending oneself and taking revenge? How did Jesus treat those who nailed Him to a cross? How are we to treat people who are not kind to us?

Older children and grownups may now read: Matthew 5:38-41.

Let us pray together: Heavenly Father, keep us from ever saying, "I will treat others the way they treat me." Help us to love those who hurt us, the way Jesus did. In Jesus' name we ask this. Amen.

110

Bless the Lord, O my soul. Psalm 103:1

What Your Soul Should Do

Do you know what kind of songbook our Lord Jesus used? He used the Book of Psalms. The Psalms are poems. Many of these poems were sung as hymns. One of them begins and ends with these words: "Bless the Lord, O my soul." What do you think that means?

"Bless the Lord" means "Thank and praise the Lord." The rest of the psalm tells why we ought to thank and praise the Lord. The main reason is that He forgives all our sins and loves us and is good to us, that's why.

Who should bless the Lord? The psalm says that my soul should. What is the soul? Suppose some dollmaker made a doll just as big as you, just as pretty as you, just as heavy as you, looking just like you. What would be the difference between you and the doll? The doll isn't alive. It has no soul.

My soul is *me* while I'm alive; your soul is *you* while you are alive! When the psalm writer said, "Bless the Lord, O my soul," he meant that he himself should thank and praise the Lord with his whole heart and life.

The Lord Jesus deserves to be thanked and praised. He saved us from being punished in hell for our sins. He died for us on a cross so that God can forgive all our sins. He loves us as a father loves his children. And someday He will take us to heaven. "Bless the Lord, O my soul."

Let's talk about this: What are the Psalms? What are the words at the beginning and end of Psalm 103? What does "bless the Lord" mean? What is our "soul"? Why do we want to bless the Lord Jesus? How can we thank and praise Him with our whole life?

111

Bible reading for older children and grownups: Psalm 103:1-5.

Let us bless the Lord: We thank and praise You, Lord Jesus, for all that You did for us and still do for us. Especially do we thank You for loving and forgiving us every day. Please help us to show that we are thankful by the way we act. Amen.

The Lord knows the thoughts of man. Psalm 94:11

God Knows What You Think

"Mother, why does God go by what we think in our hearts?" asked Ann one day.

"You would, too, if you could," said her mother.

"Would I?" asked Ann.

"I think so," said the mother. "If somebody invited you to a party, and you knew she was thinking, 'I hope Ann stays away,' would you go?"

"Oh, no," said Ann. "I wouldn't go if they didn't want me."

"And if somebody said, 'You look lovely, Ann,' but you knew that he would laugh about you later, would you be glad over what he said, or sad over what he thought?"

"I wouldn't feel so good," said Ann.

"So you see," said Ann's mother, "we would all go by what people think if we could; only we can't always see what they think. But God can, and so He knows just what we are and how we feel and what we really mean. He knows that we are often selfish and proud and foolish."

But God also knows the people who are sorry that they

sin, and He knows those who believe that Jesus died in order to save them. He forgives the wrong thinking of those who are sorry, and is happy over those who love Jesus.

Let's talk this over: Does God go by what we think or by what we say? Why do people often believe what we say? What kind of wrong thoughts do we often have? What kind of thinking does God want to see in us? What does He do with our wrong thinking when we love Jesus?

Bible reading for older children and grownups: Psalm 94:9-12.

Let us pray: Dear God, please forgive us all our sins for Jesus' sake, for who can hide anything from You? Keep us from wrong thoughts and feelings, and teach us to obey You in all things. Amen.

Do good to them that hate
    you. Matthew 5:44

How to Treat Mean Children

One day Helen said, "Mother, I will never, never again play with Gladys. She is SO bad."

"Well, my little girl wants to be a Christian, doesn't she?" said her mother.

"But, Mother, you don't know how Gladys hates me," replied Helen. "Every day she is mean to me. She always hits me when nobody is looking, and then she says she didn't do it."

"What have you tried to do to help yourself?" asked the mother.

"What can I do? She's bigger than I," said Helen.

"Why not try doing what Jesus said?" asked her mother.

113

"What did He say we should do?" asked Helen.

"He said, 'Do good to them that hate you.' Why don't you try that?" her mother told her.

So Helen tried that. She knew Gladys was saving postage stamps, so she hunted for a real good one and gave it to Gladys. She also told Gladys, "Your teeth are very pretty," because they really were.

Guess what happened! Pretty soon Gladys was good to Helen, and they became friends. On Sunday Helen brought Gladys along to church, and every Sunday after that they went together. When Gladys learned about Jesus, she said, "Now I know why you were nice to me even when I wasn't nice to you."

Let's talk about this: Why didn't Helen like Gladys at first? What did her mother say? What did Helen try? How did it turn out? The Bible tells how Jesus loved us and died for us even before we loved Him. Can you say the Bible verse which tells how to treat people who hate us?

Older children and grownups may now read: Matthew 5:43-48.

Let's pray for our enemies: Dear Jesus, please help us to love our enemies as You do. Even when children hate us and are mean to us, remind us to do good to them, for Your sake. Amen.

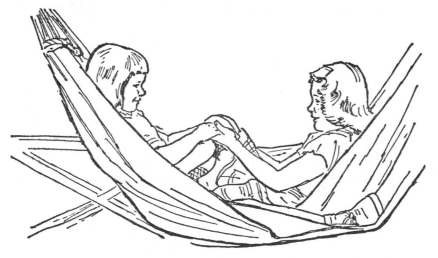

Try to learn what is pleasing to the
Lord. Ephesians 5:10 (RSV)

The Best Lesson of All

"No more lessons for a whole week," said Ray, and he was all smiles. It was time for the Easter vacation.

"Well, then, this week let's learn the best lesson of all," his father replied.

"Oh, Dad, another lesson?" grumbled Ray.

"It's an easy lesson to learn, but a hard one to do," said his father.

"All right," said Ray, a little curious. "What's the lesson?"

"It's in the Bible," said his father. "See if you can get it. In St. Paul's Letter to the Ephesians it says: 'Try to learn what is pleasing to the Lord.'"

" 'Try to learn what is pleasing to the Lord.' Is that the lesson?" asked Ray. "I know that."

"Don't be too sure," said his father. "Does your mouth always know what pleases Jesus? Do your eyes? Do your hands? Do they know it so well that they do it? It's not enough to know what is good and right and true. God wants us to learn to *do* what is pleasing to the Lord."

Let's think about this: Which lesson did Ray's father want him to learn? Why did Ray think he knew that lesson? What were some of the questions the father asked? Why did Ray still have to learn what is pleasing to the Lord? Why do we? Let's say the memory words together.

Bible reading for older children and grownups: Ephesians 5:1-10.

Let us pray: Dear God, please help us always to know what is pleasing to You, and make us glad and able to do it. In Jesus' name we ask this. Amen.

115

God's Word is a lamp unto
   my feet. Psalm 119:105

The Best Flashlight

"Mother, it's dark outside," said Kathy, "I can't see, and I want to go to the garage." She had left her library book in the car.

"Take this flashlight, Honey," said her mother. "It will show you the way."

So Kathy took the flashlight, and then it was easy to see the way. She could also see where not to go. Wherever she pointed the flashlight, the light would shine. It helped her get to the garage and safely back to the house.

"What do you think is the best flashlight in the world?" asked Kathy's father when she came back. She was swinging her light around the kitchen. "I'll give you a hint," he said. "It's called a lamp instead of a flashlight."

"I know," said Kathy. " 'Thy Word is a lamp unto my feet and a light unto my path.' King David said that. He meant the Bible."

"That's right," said Kathy's daddy. "In the days when King David lived, people didn't have flashlights. They had little lamps which they carried when they went somewhere in the dark. In what way is God's Word like a lamp or a flashlight?"

Kathy thought a while. "Well," she said, "the flashlight helped me to see the way in the dark. The light also kept me from falling over something and getting hurt."

"Right again," said her dad. He was very happy to see that his girl was doing some thinking. "And the Bible shows us the way to get to heaven and keeps us from getting lost or hurting ourselves. By the way," he said, "what does the Bible say is the only way to get to heaven?"

"That's easy," said Kathy. "By believing that Jesus is our Savior. The Bible says, 'He that believeth and is baptized shall be saved; but he that believeth not shall be damned.'"

Let's talk about this: What are flashlights good for? What did King David use instead of a flashlight? What did King David call God's Word? In which way is the Bible like a lamp or flashlight? The Bible shows us the only way to heaven. What is it? The Bible also keeps us from stumbling along the way. We stumble whenever we sin. How does God's Word keep us from sinning? Let's say the Bible verse together.

Older children and grownups may now read: Psalm 119:97-104.

Let us pray together: Dear Lord, we're glad that we have Your Word as a light to show us the way to heaven and a lamp to keep us from sinning. Please let it shine brightly for us, for Jesus' sake. Amen.

Pleasant words are like a honeycomb, sweet to the soul and health to the bones. Proverbs 16:24

Some Words Are like Medicine

"I'm a doctor," said Elaine; "Grandma said so."

"Why did she say you were a doctor?" Elaine's mother asked her.

"Grandma said, 'When you come, it's like good medicine.' I tell her nice things, and it makes her happy," answered Elaine.

"Well, maybe you *are* a good doctor for her," said her mother. "I know a Bible verse about pleasant words. It says that pleasant words are like honey, which is good for a person."

"Tell me the verse," said Elaine.

"Pleasant words are like a honeycomb, sweet to the soul and health to the bones," said her mother. "In another place the Bible says, 'A good word makes the heart glad,' and 'A merry heart does good like a medicine.'"

Pleasant words *are* like good medicine. When a person is feeling blue and you say some friendly words to him, it cheers him up and makes him feel better.

Once there was a grouchy old woman cleaning rooms in a motel. One of the friendly guests told her, "I'm glad you keep things so clean. You do your work quickly, too."

The old woman smiled. "I don't hear things like that very often," she said. For many weeks those words were like good medicine for her. They made her feel good.

So let's not forget to say pleasant words to people. Jesus wants us to. And it's an easy way to love and help people.

Let's talk about this: Why did Grandma say that Elaine was a doctor? What do pleasant words do for a person?

What does our Bible verse say about pleasant words? When is it hard to find pleasant words to say to other people? When is it easy? Why does Jesus want us to speak pleasant words?

Bible reading for older children and grownups: Proverbs 16:23-29.

Let us pray together: Dear Father in heaven, Your words are so often like honey, sweet and good, and ours are so often like vinegar. Help us to make the hearts of other people glad, especially by telling them about their Savior Jesus. We ask this in Jesus' name. Amen.

Walk in love, as Christ has loved us. Ephesians 5:2

How to Walk in Love

Benny and Tom were walking down the street together. They started pushing each other off the sidewalk in fun. But soon Tom began to get angry. Down the street was a new lawn. It was muddy. It had just been planted and soaked with water. When the boys were passing it, Tom pushed Benny into the mud.

Now Benny became angry. He threw some mud at Tom. Tom began to call his friend some dirty names. Benny chased Tom down the street with a rock. The two boys weren't friends any more.

If Jesus had been walking with Tom and Benny and had been a boy, what would He have done? Maybe He would have pushed a little, too. But He would have watched to see if it was really fun for Ben and Tom. If anyone began to get angry, He would have stopped pushing. And He surely would not have pushed Ben into the mud. Maybe He would have said, "Pushing people leads to quarrels." Then He would not have pushed at all.

"What would Jesus do?" That's a good question to ask often as we walk along through life. The Bible says, "Walk in love, as Christ has loved us." Our whole life is like a walk to heaven. On the way we sometimes forget to walk like Christians. Then it helps us to think of Jesus walking along with us. What would Jesus do? He would love.

"Walk in love, as Christ has loved us." How did Jesus Christ love us? The Bible says, "He has given Himself for us as an offering and as a sacrifice to God." He gave up His life for us so that God would forgive us and keep us as His children. When we love as Jesus has loved us, we forget about ourselves, and we try to please God by doing things for others.

Let's talk about this: If Jesus had been Tom walking along with Benny, what would He have done? What happened because Tom and Benny were not walking in love? When the Bible says, "Walk in love," what does this mean? What has Jesus done for us? Why did He do it? How much, then, are we to love others?

Older children and grownups may now read: Ephesians 5:1, 2.

Let us pray together: Dear Jesus, please walk with us every day on our way to heaven. Help us to learn from You how to walk in love, and forgive us when we forget. We ask this as Your children and followers. Amen.

*I will show you my faith
by my works.* James 2:18

Let's See What You Believe

Mr. Green was coming out of a tavern, half drunk. Just then the pastor came along. He said, "Mr. Green, do you think you are a Christian?" Mr. Green got angry. He took off his coat and was going to fight the pastor. "I'll show you that I'm a Christian," he said.

Is fighting a way to show others that you are a Christian? No, the more you fight, the fewer people will think that you are a Christian. Christians are people who believe in Jesus and love Him. They have faith in Jesus. They believe that He is their Lord and Savior. They trust in Him. They want Him to live in their hearts.

But how can you show your faith? How can you prove that you believe what you say you believe? How can you see whether some other person has Jesus in his heart?

James, one of the disciples of Jesus, wrote in the Bible, "I will show you my faith by my works." A person shows what he believes by what he does. Jesus said, "By this shall all men know that you are My disciples, if you have love one to another."

But James wanted us to remember another lesson. Suppose you would see somebody who didn't have enough clothes and had nothing to eat, and you had extra clothes and extra food. Suppose you said to the person, "I love you. I hope you will get some clothes and food." If you didn't give him anything, would he think you really loved him?

James said, "I will show you my faith by my works." He meant that people will be able to see by what we do whether

121

we love them. They will also be able to see by what we do whether we love Jesus.

Let's talk this over: How was Mr. Green going to make the pastor think that he was a Christian? Why is that not a good way to show that we love Jesus? What is a good way to show other people that we are disciples of Jesus?

Bible reading for older children and grownups: James 2:14-18.

Let us pray together: Lord Jesus, we believe that You are our God and our loving Savior. Forgive us for not always showing that we believe this. Help us to show our faith in You by whatever we do, and remind us to love people by helping them. Amen.

Let no evil talk come out of your mouth,
  but only that which is good. Ephesians 4:29

Is Your Mouth Clean?

"Mary, what time is it?" asked Mary's mother.

"Mmmmmmmmmm" is all Mary said.

"What on earth?" said her mother when she turned around and saw Mary's mouth taped shut with tape.

Mary took off part of the tape so she could explain. "You said I ought to tape my mouth shut when I want to say bad words."

"So you taped it shut," said her mother, and they both laughed. "Did it keep you from saying something bad?" asked her mother.

"Yes, but not from thinking bad words," said Mary. "Bruce hid my doll again, and I felt like pulling out his hair and calling him names."

122

"St. Paul wrote in the Bible, 'Let no evil talk come out of your mouth, but only that which is good,'" said Mary's mother. "I'm glad you tried to keep evil talk from coming out of your mouth, but I'm afraid something else besides tape is needed."

Mary said, "If I could stop *thinking* evil things, then I would never *say* evil things, would I, Mother?"

"That's about the way it is," said her mother. "It takes thinking to live like a Christian. And Jesus will help you to say only that which is good if you will try to be like Him. Remember, He always loved people and was holy and good. No mean and dirty talk ever came out of His mouth."

Let's talk about this: Why did Mary tape her mouth shut? Did it stop her from *thinking* bad words? Where must we stop bad words, at the mouth or in the heart? Which Bible verse did Mary's mother tell her? Who will help us to say only that which is good?

Older children and grownups may now read: Ephesians 4:28-32.

Let us pray for clean hearts and mouths: Dear Father in heaven, please forgive the many times when we have forgotten that we are Your children and have let mean or dirty talk come out of our mouths. Make our hearts clean so that our talking will always be good instead of evil. We ask this in Jesus' name. Amen.

*Thou, O Lord, art good and ready
to forgive.* Psalm 86:5

What God Is Ready to Do

Sammy had an awful toothache. His mother told him to go to the dentist instead of to school. So he did.

When Sammy got there, the waiting room was full of people. "The dentist can't see you today," said the nurse.

"But it hurts very much," said Sam.

"Oh, does it?" she said. Then she went and talked to the dentist. The dentist came to the door and said to Sam, "Come right in, my boy. If you have a bad toothache, I'm ready to help you."

That night Sammy told his folks how good the dentist was. "He helped me right away because I needed help," said Sammy.

"Why, that's just the way God helps us all the time," said Sammy's father. "He is always ready to forgive us. 'Thou, Lord, art good and ready to forgive,' said King David in a psalm."

"I'm glad we don't have to wait in a big waiting room every time we want God to forgive us," said Sammy.

"Yes," said his dad. "We need God's forgiveness every day. The Lord is ready to forgive all who ask Him. He doesn't even wait to be asked. When we want His forgiveness, He gives it to us all the time. That's why King David was happy, and we ought to be, too."

"Do you know why God is always ready to forgive us?" asked Sammy's mother.

"Sure," answered Sammy, "on account of Jesus. Jesus asked God to do it and paid for our sins." Sammy was right.

124

Let's talk about this: Why did Sammy think the dentist was a good man? Why did King David call God good? Why do we need God's forgiveness every day? For whose sake is God ready to forgive us? How did Sammy feel when he thought about God's forgiveness? Let's say the Bible verse together.

Bible reading for older children and grownups: Psalm 86:3-7.

Let us pray together: Dear Lord God, we are glad that You are always ready to forgive us even before we come and ask You for mercy. Please forgive us all our sins this day, and keep us as Your children for Jesus' sake. Amen.

When you have shut your door, pray to your Father who is in secret. Matthew 6:6

Places to Pray

"Mother, I found a good place to pray," said Dan when he came home from school one day.

"Where?" his mother asked.

"On the bus. When it's crowded with people, nobody pays any attention to you. I sat there and did what our pastor told us to do: I went around the world praying."

"How did you do that?" asked his mother.

"I thought about the missionaries in Japan, and asked God to bless them. Then I remembered the poor refugees in Hong Kong, and I prayed for them. Then I hopped to Africa and then to the Philippines and then to Mexico and —"

"You did this on the crowded bus?" his mother asked. She was a little surprised.

"Sure," said Dan. "I also pray when I'm delivering my

papers. My Sunday school teacher told me that houses without Christians in them are always dark. So when I know that the people in a house do not go to church, I ask Jesus to turn His light on in their house."

"Any place is a good place to pray," said his mother. "Jesus said we should shut our door and pray in secret. He meant we should not pray to show off. But we can talk to our Father in heaven all by ourselves, anywhere and anytime, without anybody knowing it."

Let's talk about this: How did Dan pray around the world on a bus one day? For whom did Dan pray when he delivered papers? Why did Jesus tell us to pray in secret? Does God care where we pray? Where can a person pray to God in secret by himself?

Older children and grownups may now read: Matthew 6:5-8.

Let us pray together: Dear heavenly Father, we are glad that we can talk to You in any place at any time. Please keep us from ever showing off when we pray. Help us to pray to You in our hearts even when we are all praying together. We ask this in Jesus' name. Amen.

*The earth is full of the goodness
of the Lord.* Psalm 33:5

The Lord Is Good

"Isn't the grass pretty? Jesus makes the grass green," a mother told her little boy Mark.

"Why does Jesus make the grass green?" asked Mark.

"Oh," she said, "'cause He's good. He's the One who also made the sky blue."

"Why did Jesus make the sky blue?" asked little Mark.

"Well," his mother explained, "you wouldn't like to have a black sky or black grass or black flowers or black snow, would you?"

The Bible says, "The earth is full of the goodness of the Lord." Everything God has made in the world shows how good He is. When the sun starts to shine through the clouds on a cold day, we say, "How good the sun feels." Without the sun nothing could live. When the sun gets too hot and clouds cover it and send rain to cool off the ground, we say, "How good the rain is." God gives us the sunshine and the rain.

127

But the easiest way to see that the Lord is good is to remember what Jesus has done for us and what He promises us in the Bible. He died on a cross for us and for all people, and He promises to take all of His children to heaven. He didn't have to do that. It's only because He's so good.

Let's think about this: What color would you choose for grass? Why would black not be good? Why did Jesus make the world beautiful? What's so good about sunshine? Why does He send us rain? What are some other good things that God gives us? What's the easiest way to see that the Lord Jesus loves us? Let's say the Bible verse together.

Bible reading for older children and grownups: Psalm 33:1-8.

Now let us praise the Lord for His goodness: Lord Jesus, our God and Savior, we thank and praise You for making the world and all that is in it bright and good and beautiful. But most of all we thank You for saving us and making us God's children. Amen.

You shall be witnesses. Acts 1:8

What Jesus Wants Us to Be

Have you ever seen a courtroom where they try to find out the truth about people who are caught by the police?

There is a judge in a black gown, sitting behind a table on a platform. There is the person who is brought before the judge. There is a policeman. There is a witness telling what he knows. There is a lawyer asking questions and arguing.

Jesus said that His people should be like one of those five persons. Do you know which one? He did not say we

128

should be policemen, ordering people to do what's right. He doesn't want us to be judges, who punish people. He didn't say we should be lawyers who argue with people. And He surely doesn't want us to be the people who do wrong.

Jesus said, "You are to be witnesses for Me." A witness tells what he knows. Some people believe him, some people don't, but that doesn't matter. He just tells what he knows.

What are we to tell? We are to tell people what we know about Jesus. We are to tell anyone who doesn't know about Him. Some will believe; some won't believe; but that doesn't matter. We are to be witnesses.

A witness is expected to tell the truth, the whole truth, and nothing but the truth. The truth about Jesus is in the Bible. The truth is that He is God's Son and the Savior of the world.

Have you ever told someone else about Jesus? Did you tell the truth? Then you were a good witness. Remember that Jesus wants you to be a witness for Him. Watch for a chance to speak up for Him every day. Let's say the Bible verse together.

Let's talk about this: What did Jesus say we should be? What does a witness do in a courtroom? When are we witnesses for Jesus? What could you tell about Jesus? Do you know anyone who needs to be told about Jesus?

Older children and grownups may now read: Acts 1:7-9.

Let us pray: Dear Jesus, please help us all to learn more about You and about God's Word. Make us good witnesses. We want to tell others the truth about You. Help them to believe us so that they will love You. Amen.

*If you know these things, happy are you
if you do them.*   John 13:17

Knowing and Doing

"I know the most Bible verses in my class," said Betty. Then, after thinking a bit, she asked, "Mother, does that make me the best Christian in my class?"

Mother sat down with Betty. "Darling," she said, "I hope all of the boys and girls in your class are very, very good and that you are the best Christian of them all. But knowing some Bible verses may not even make a person a Christian at all, let alone a good Christian."

"But I learned them to please Jesus," said Betty.

"Then they show that you love Jesus and that you want to be a good Christian," said her mother. "But there's a big difference between knowing and doing. Which Bible verses do you know?"

Betty said, "I know 'Trust in the Lord with all thine heart' and 'Let not your heart be troubled, neither let it be afraid' and a lot more."

"Well," said her mother, "do you always believe that the Lord Jesus loves you and is with you all the time, and do you trust that He can and will take care of you?"

"N-no, not always," Betty admitted; "I still worry a lot, don't I?"

"I'm afraid so," said her mother with a smile. "What other verse do you know?"

" 'This is My Commandment, that ye love one another as I have loved you.' Jesus said that," Betty told her mother.

"I'm glad you know that verse," said her mother. "But how about the doing? Do you always love Tom the way Jesus loves you?" Betty often quarreled with her brother Tom.

"No, Mother," said Betty. "I guess just knowing Bible verses doesn't make me a good Christian. But if I'll remember to *do* them, I'll be a better Christian, won't I?"

"Yes," said her mother, "and Jesus said, 'If you know these things, happy are you if you do them.' The more you really do whatever the Bible tells you, the happier you will be."

Let's talk about this: Was Betty the best Christian because she knew the most Bible verses? Why not? What were some of the verses Betty knew but didn't always do? What Bible words do we know but may not always do? Why is it good to know Bible verses? Do all who know Bible verses do them? What did Jesus say will make us happy?

Bible reading for older children and grownups: John 13:12-17.

Let us pray together: Dear Jesus, please help us to know the things You have taught, and help us also to do them so that we will be happy Christians. Amen.

The Lord, our God, is holy. Psalm 99:9

Our Holy God

"Holy, holy, holy, Lord God almighty." Jim and Judy were singing as loudly as they could. They were playing church on the porch steps. Jim was the preacher.

"I will now tell you why God is holy," Jim began saying to Judy. But then he didn't know how to go on. So he ran into the house to his mother.

"Mother, what is holy?" he asked.

"God is holy," she said. "That means, God has no sin. God never does anything wrong. Everything God does is just right."

"Are you holy, Mother?" Jim asked.

"Oh, no," she said. "We all do things that we shouldn't do, and often we don't do what we ought to do. But God always does only what is good. He is holy. He is perfect."

"God's angels are holy," said Jim, remembering what he had heard in Sunday school.

"Yes," said his mother, "but people aren't holy. They do wrong things. You do naughty things sometimes, don't you? Because all people sin, they are not holy. They need God's forgiveness."

"But aren't we holy when God forgives us?" asked Jim.

"Yes, that's right," said his mother. "Jesus washes away all sins and makes us holy. But only God is holy in what He does."

Jim went outside to tell Judy.

Let's talk about this: What were Jim and Judy playing? What hymn were they singing? What does "holy" mean? Who else is holy besides God? What keeps us from being holy? How can people become holy? How does God expect His holy children to act? Let's say the Bible verse together.

Bible reading for older children and grownups: Isaiah 6:1-8.

Let us pray: Dear heavenly Father, we are glad that You never do anything wrong and always do what is right and good. Please make us holy by forgiving all our sins for Jesus' sake. Then help us to be good by giving us the Holy Spirit in our hearts. We ask this in Jesus' name. Amen.

When I am afraid, I will trust in God. Psalm 56:3

What to Do When Afraid

Billy and Peg had played in the schoolyard too long. Now it was getting dark, and they had to walk past a cemetery to get home. There were dead people buried in the cemetery. Their friend Jackie had said, "There are ghosts in the cemetery."

So Billy and Peg were a little afraid.

"Mother told us there are no ghosts in the cemetery," said Peg. But Peg wasn't so sure. Her eyes were blinking fast.

"I know it," said Billy, trying to act brave. "But at night-time everything looks so spooky. Maybe something is hiding in there."

"I know what let's do," said Peg. "Let's pray to Jesus to go with us." So they stopped and folded their hands. Peg said, "Dear Jesus, be with us on our way home." Then they started walking again.

"If Jesus is with us, we don't have to be afraid," said Billy, feeling better.

"But Jesus is with us all the time, so we never have to be afraid," said Peg. "I'm glad Jesus is always with us," she added.

"So am I," said Billy. " 'When I am afraid, I will trust in God.' That's what I learned to say from the Bible."

"When I am afraid, I will trust in God," said Peg. "That's what I'm going to say the next time I'm afraid."

Let's talk about this: Why were Billy and Peg afraid? Are there ghosts in some cemeteries? Do we ever have to be afraid if Jesus is with us? Which verse in the Bible did Billy and Peg say? Why will Jesus protect also us?

133

Older children and grownups may now read: Psalm 56:3, 4, 9-11.

Let us pray together: Dear Jesus, thank You for being with us and for loving us all the time and for taking care of us. Please help us to trust in You always and to love You, because You love us and are our dear Savior and God. Amen.

You are the light of the world. Matthew 5:14

Are You a Shining Example?

"Get the lamp, Daddy; the lights are out," said Freddie. They had an old lamp in a closet. There was oil in the lamp and a piece of cloth which burned and made some light. Freddie's dad put the lamp on the table, and it brightened up the whole room.

"You know, Freddie," said his father, "that lamp isn't quite like the lamps they had in the days when Jesus lived on earth, but it reminds me of what Jesus said about His people being lights. Do you know the words I mean?"

134

"You are the light of the world," said Freddie. "Is that it?"

"Yes, that's the verse I mean," said his father. "All those who know Jesus and trust that Jesus is their Savior are like a lamp that gives light. They tell others about Jesus and show them the way to heaven. They also brighten up other people's lives by what they do."

"That isn't a very strong light; and look how it flickers," said Freddie.

"That's just like most of us," said his dad. "We aren't very good Christians either, and so our light flickers. But the more lamps there are in a place, the brighter the light is."

"Oh, boy, if we had a hundred lamps, we would really have a big light," said Freddie. "And if every light would shine brightly, that would make the light real bright, wouldn't it!"

"Yes," said his dad. "Don't forget: You are the light of the world. You and all the people who believe in Jesus."

Let's talk about this: Why is a Christian like a lamp? What can a Christian help other people see? Sometimes our light is brighter than at other times. When is it real bright? Let's say the Bible verse together.

Bible reading for older children and grownups: Matthew 5:14-16.

Let us pray: Dear Lord Jesus, help us to shine brightly as Christians in all that we say and do. We want others around us to see how good You are. Then they may believe that You are the Savior of the world and will also follow You and be saved. Amen.

The Lord is . . . slow to anger and plenteous in mercy. Psalm 103:8

In What God Is Slow

"Look how fast God makes the lightning go," said Tim. He was watching it go across the sky. Sometimes it went so fast he couldn't see where it started or where it ended. "God sure can do things fast," said Tim.

"You bet," said his father. "God can do anything in a second. Remember how He made the world? He just said, 'Let there be plants and trees,' and there they were, and, 'Let there be animals,' and there they were. He could blow up the whole world in a minute if He wanted to," said Tim's father.

But God is slow about one thing. The Bible says, "The Lord is . . . slow to anger." Even though we all sin every day, He doesn't "fly off the handle" at us. He doesn't punish us as we deserve right away. No, He is very patient with us. It takes Him a long time to get angry at a person.

The Bible tells us why God is slow in getting angry. It's because He is so kind and full of love. "The Lord is . . . plenteous in mercy," says the psalm writer. That means He is full of mercy. For Jesus' sake He does not treat us as we deserve, but He forgives us all our sins.

How wonderfully good our God is. That is why the psalm writer also says, "Bless the Lord, O my soul; and all that is within me, bless His holy name."

Let's talk about this: What made Tim think that God does things fast? In what is God very slow? Why is the Lord slow in getting angry at us? Why is it a good thing that God is slow in getting angry? For whose sake is He full of mercy and kind and forgiving? Who can say the Bible verse?

Older children and grownups may now read: Psalm 103:8-13.

Let us bow and pray: Dear Lord God, how glad we are that You are slow to anger and that You are willing to forgive us our sins for Jesus' sake. Help us to be kind and forgiving with other people and slow in getting angry at them. We ask this in Jesus' name. Amen.

Jesus said, I am the Good Shepherd. John 10:14

The Lord Is My Shepherd

Once there was a man who had 100 sheep. One evening he counted them as they went into the gate. Only 99 were there! One was missing! It must not have followed the shepherd and was lost in the dark woods.

At once the man closed the gate and left his helpers to watch the sheep. He must find the lost lamb before some wolf or lion would get her. He hurried to the places where the sheep had been that day, and he called the sheep's name.

For a while the shepherd heard nothing. Again and again he called. At last he heard a weak "Baa." Before long he found her, all tangled up in some bushes. He pulled her out, but she couldn't walk; she had hurt her leg. So he carried her home on his shoulders.

137

"Look," he called to the other shepherds as he came back, "I found my sheep which was lost." They all were happy with him.

This shepherd is somebody we know. It is Jesus. And we are the sheep. Sometimes we are like a little lost lamb. When we sin, we go down a wrong path away from God. But Jesus is always calling us back. He wants us all to be safe with Him. And He is very happy over all who are saved. "I am the Good Shepherd," said Jesus. The Good Shepherd even gave His life for the sheep.

Let's talk about this: Why did the man leave his 99 sheep? What had happened to the lamb that was missing? How did the shepherd bring the lost lamb home? Why was the shepherd glad? Who is the shepherd Jesus was talking about? Who are Jesus' sheep? When are we like the little lost lamb? Why is Jesus called "the good Shepherd"?

Older children and grownups may now read: Luke 15:3-7.

Let us pray: Dear Jesus, our Good Shepherd, we are glad that we are Your sheep and lambs. Please keep us close to You every day. If ever we become lost by forgetting You, please call us and save us. Keep us always with You here on earth so that we will be with You in heaven. Amen.

*Jesus said, Blessed are
the merciful.* Matthew 5:7

Feeling Sorry for Other People

"I feel so sorry for Mrs. Jacobs," said Margaret. "She is very poor, and now she is in the hospital. Her children haven't any daddy, and they're home all alone, and they probably don't have anything to eat."

"I'm glad you feel that way, Margaret," said Mrs. Smith. "Jesus said, 'Blessed are the merciful.'"

"Does merciful mean being sorry for other people?" asked Margaret.

"Yes," said her mother, "sorry enough to do something about it."

"What can we do?" asked Margaret.

"Well," said her mother. "We could start by making a chocolate cake for the children. Do you think they would like that?"

"Oh, yes," said Margaret.

So Mrs. Smith made a cake, and Margaret carried it over to Mrs. Jacobs' house. Mrs. Smith went along to see if there was anything that she could do for the children. She also brought them a loaf of bread and some butter and five cans of soup and some eggs.

At supper that night the Smith family talked some more about Mrs. Jacobs' troubles. Mr. Smith said, "I think I'll write a card to everybody living around here. I'll tell them I'm coming Saturday to collect money to help Mrs. Jacobs." And that's just what he did.

When Mr. Smith talked to the neighbors the next Saturday, most of them were glad to help Mrs. Jacobs. All together they gave enough to pay for her hospital bill. When Mrs. Jacobs heard about it, she cried and thanked God for people who are merciful.

"Blessed are the merciful, for they shall receive mercy," said Jesus. Those who love Jesus and are kind and helpful are happy people. They receive much love and kindness from God.

Let's talk about this: How did Margaret show that she was merciful? What did her mother do for Mrs. Jacobs' children? What did Mr. Smith do to help Mrs. Jacobs? Jesus said that merciful people are blessed and happy. What do they receive from God? Let's say the Bible verse together.

Bible reading for older children and grownups: 1 John 3:16-18.

Let us thank God for HIS mercy: Thank You, dear heavenly Father, for always feeling sorry for us and giving us so many blessings which we do not deserve. Especially do we thank You for forgiving us all our sins. Help us to be merciful to people as You are merciful to us. In Jesus' name we ask this. Amen.

140

*The Lord will hear when I call
to Him.* Psalm 4:3

God Listens to His Children

Have you ever been in trouble, real bad trouble, when you didn't know what to do?

King David had many troubles. Before he became king, David had to run away from Saul, who was trying to kill him. Later David had to run away from Absalom, his own son. Absalom tried to get rid of his father so that he could be the king.

Usually our troubles come from our sins. When we have told a lie, when we have broken a window, when we have been mean, when we forget to do our duty, we get into trouble. Some of King David's troubles were his own fault.

But sometimes we get into trouble even when we haven't done anything wrong. Maybe somebody gets sick, or we lose our money, or we fall and get dirty, or somebody is mean to us. There are many different kinds of troubles in the world.

What can we do whenever we are in trouble? We can pray to God. We can say what King David said. He said, "Hear me when I call, O God. . . . Have mercy upon me and hear my prayer."

King David knew that God would help him. He said, "The Lord will hear when I call to Him." So he prayed to God often, and then he stopped worrying.

We know that God loves all people, especially His children. We, too, can say, "The Lord will hear when I call to Him." So let's not forget to ask God for help when we're in trouble. He will help us for Jesus' sake.

Let's talk about prayer: What did King David believe the Lord would do for him? What kind of troubles do children have sometimes? What kind of troubles do grownups have? Why is it foolish not to ask God for help in times of trouble? Why are people happy when they trust in God?

Bible reading for older children and grownups: Psalm 4:3-8.

Let us pray: Dear God, we are glad that You are willing to help us in any trouble, and we thank You for Your promises to hear our prayers. Hear our prayers for the sake of Jesus, our dear Savior. Amen.

Trust in the Lord. Proverbs 3:5

Why Little Joe Didn't Worry

"I don't know what we'll do this week," said Mr. Andrews to his wife at the supper table. "I won't get paid until Friday, and we haven't any money for food."

"Jesus can help us," said little Joe. Joe was one of Mr. Andrews' six children. He said, "Jesus once made a boy's lunch enough for many people."

"You're right, Joey," said Mrs. Andrews, "let's ask Jesus to help us." So Mr. Andrews prayed, "Dear Jesus, please help us to get enough food for this week." Mrs. Andrews and the children prayed along, too.

That evening the telephone rang. It was the man who owned the grocery store on the corner. He said, "I wonder if you could use some cans of food." He knew that the Andrews family was large. "I had some cans outside and didn't notice that it started to rain," he said. "All the paper came off the cans, so I can't very well sell them. Could you use them?"

142

"Could I use them?" shouted Mr. Andrews. "You're the answer to my prayer."

"Trust in the Lord," said his wife when he told her about the groceryman. "Jesus always finds a way to help us when we depend on Him."

Little Joe was right. Jesus always has a way to help us. There is no trouble in which He can't help us. Sometimes He doesn't help us right away. That's so we will learn for sure that we can trust Him. Sometimes He waits till nothing else can help us so that we will know He was the One who did it.

We can always be sure that Jesus can help us. He does, too, when we depend on Him. "Trust in the Lord," says the Bible. To trust means to believe that He will do what He has promised.

Let's talk about this: Why was Mr. Andrews worried? What did his little boy Joe tell him? What happened when they prayed to Jesus? Why doesn't Jesus always help right away? What does it mean to "trust in the Lord"?

Bible reading for older children and grownups: Proverbs 3:1-6.

Let us pray to Jesus: It is wonderful to know that we can always depend on You, dear Jesus. Please help us to remember this especially when we're in trouble. We thank You and love You for having saved us from sin, our worst trouble. Please keep us in Your kingdom and bless us. Amen.

My help comes from the Lord, who made heaven and earth. Psalm 121:2

The Best Helper in the World

"Who helps God when He needs help?" Tommy asked his dad one day.

"God never needs help," his father answered. "God can do anything. He is the almighty Maker of heaven and earth. If He needed anything, He could make it just by wanting it."

"Oh," said Tommy. After thinking a while he added, "Boy, then God can always help us."

Tommy got it right, didn't he? Sometimes boys and girls may ask their father or mother for something, but their parents cannot help them. When Tommy was sick, he asked his father to help him get better, but his father couldn't do much for him. But God always can help us. He can do anything. He made heaven and earth.

The Bible verse says, "My help comes from the Lord, who made heaven and earth." Psalm 121 also says that the Lord never sleeps, and He watches over His children and keeps them from harm.

That is why the psalm writer said, "I will lift up mine eyes." He meant that he would look up to heaven for whatever help he needed, because the Lord, who is in heaven, could help him and would help him. Let us do the same, because Jesus, our Lord, loves us and can and will help us.

Let's talk about this: What was Tommy wondering one day? Why doesn't God ever need help? Why are we glad that our Helper is the almighty Maker of heaven and earth? What did the psalm writer mean when he said he would lift up his eyes to the Lord? Why are we foolish if we do

144

not ask God to take care of us? Let's say the Bible verse together.

Older children and grownups may now read: Psalm 121.

Let us pray together: Dear heavenly Father, we are glad that we have been made Your children by Jesus, our Savior. For His sake, please love us and keep us, and teach us to trust in Your help at all times. Amen.

Forget not all His benefits. Psalm 103:2

Reasons for Being Thankful

"How thankful I am!" said Mrs. Smith. "My boy was driving on Banner Road. He fell asleep and drove down a steep bank. The car rolled over twice, but he wasn't hurt. Isn't it wonderful how God kept him from harm?"

"Yes, it certainly is," said Miss Brown. "God was good to your boy. But He keeps us from harm every day," she said.

"How is that?" asked Mrs. Smith.

"I drive on Banner Road ten times a week," said Miss Brown. "I've never fallen asleep while driving; I've never run down the bank and never wrecked the car. Don't you think that's even more wonderful?"

Mrs. Smith smiled. "I guess we forget about God's care until we have an accident like my boy had. We really ought to thank God more when no troubles come to us. But even troubles are blessings for God's children."

"Yes," said Miss Brown, "and the Bible says, 'Forget not all His benefits.'"

Let's talk about this: If a blind man were able to see again, how would he feel? Would he be getting more blessings from God than we get? Why might he be more thankful for his eyes than we are? Do we thank God as much as we should? Can you think of some things that happened lately for which we ought to thank God?

Older children and grownups may now read: Ps. 103:1-4.

Let us thank God for His daily care: Thank You, dear Father in heaven, for all the love and care which You give us every day of our lives. Thank You for being so good to us even though we forget You so much. Please forgive us when we forget You. Keep us safe in Your love always, for Jesus' sake. Amen.

Even the winds and the sea obey Him. Matthew 8:27

Our Lord Is Mighty

There was a big storm on the lake. The wind was strong, and big waves were splashing over the boat. Water was coming into the boat faster than the men could scoop it out. Jesus was asleep at one end of the boat. His friends woke Him. They said, "Lord, save us." They thought they were going to drown soon.

Jesus got up and talked to the wind and the water. He told them to be quiet. Right away the wind was quiet, and the water quit splashing. The friends of Jesus were surprised. They said, "What kind of man is this? Even the winds and the sea obey Him!"

146

Just think! Jesus can talk to the wind and tell it to be quiet, and it quits blowing. He can tell the thunder to quit rolling or the rain to quit falling or the fire to quit burning or the sickness to quit hurting. Everything has to do what Jesus tells it to do.

Well, then, why doesn't Jesus chase away all of our troubles? Well, often we don't ask Him to do so. And sometimes when we ask Him, He knows it is better not to do what we want.

A man once asked Jesus to help him catch a train. But when he got to the station, the train was gone. Afterwards the man heard that the train had crashed into another train. Then the man was glad he had missed the train.

If Jesus wants to, He can do anything. Doctors said Jim could never get well again. Jim said to Jesus: "I am willing to be sick, if You want me to be sick, dear Jesus. But if it will be good for me, please make me well. The doctors don't think I can get well, but I know You can talk to the sickness, and it has to obey You." And Jesus did make Jimmy well. The doctors were surprised.

Let's talk about this: What was the wind doing on the lake? Who was in a boat? Why did they wake Jesus? What did Jesus tell the wind? What happened when Jesus told the wind to be still? What can Jesus say to our troubles? Why does Jesus not always chase our troubles away? When will He take all of our troubles away?

Bible reading for older children and adults: Matthew 8:23-27.

Let us pray together: Dear Jesus, help us to believe that You have power over all things, and teach us to pray to You in time of trouble. But since You know what is best for us, please do not give us what we want unless it will be good for us. We know that You love us, and we love you. Amen.

147

My thoughts are not your thoughts,
says the Lord. Isaiah 55:8

The Best Thoughts

"I prayed to God for sunshine on my birthday, but it's raining," said Johnny. "Why didn't God answer my prayer?"

His mother said, "Johnny, two boys dug up some ground one day. One planted a garden and the other collected some worms. That night the boy with the garden prayed for rain. The other boy prayed for sunshine so he could go fishing. What would you have expected God to do?"

"I don't know," said Johnny.

"Wouldn't it be better for us just to tell God what we want and then to be glad that He decides what is best? Maybe other people needed rain on your birthday. God does not always think the way we think, and He doesn't always do what we want, but His ways are always best," said his mother.

"My thoughts are not your thoughts, says the Lord." He has much better thoughts than we. He shows this by gladly

148

forgiving the sins of all who ask Him for mercy. He does this for Jesus' sake. We would not think that He would do this if He had not told us. We can be glad that God does not think the way we do.

Let's talk about this: Whose ways of thinking are always better than ours? How do we think all bad people should be treated? What is God's way of treating us? For whose sake does He love us? Where can we find out what some of God's thoughts are? Let's say the Bible verse together.

Older children and grownups may now read: Isaiah 55:6-9.

Let us pray together: Dear Father in heaven, please forgive us for not always believing that what You do is best. We know that You love us and that all Your thoughts are good. Help us to remember that You are always willing to have us as Your dear children for Jesus' sake. Amen.

Lord, if You want to, You can make me clean. Mark 1:40

What Jesus Can Do for Us

He was a big man, but he cried that day when he found out he had leprosy. Leprosy was something no doctor could heal at that time. A leper had to live outside of his city with other lepers and beg for money to buy things to eat. He would build himself a little house out of mud and sticks, and wait to die.

But someone must have told the man, "Jesus has been healing lepers and has been doing many other wonderful things. People say that He is the Son of God and the Savior God promised to send."

149

The leper believed that Jesus could help him. He hoped Jesus would soon come to his city. Then maybe Jesus would heal him. Maybe. Otherwise he could never be healed.

One day the leper heard that Jesus was coming to his city. So he stood as near to the gate as he dared, and waited. At last Jesus came. There were many people with him. The leper ran to Jesus, nearer than the Law said he could. He kneeled down in front of Jesus and said, "Lord, if You want to, You can make me clean."

Jesus felt very sorry for the poor man. He even touched him. Nobody had touched him for a long time, because people were afraid of catching his sickness. Jesus touched him and said, "I want to help you. You are clean."

All at once his sore spots left him, his skin became smooth and clean, and he was healthy and strong again.

We don't have leprosy, but we have the sickness of sin, which is worse. And no one can take away all the badness in our heart except Jesus. But like the leper we can say to Jesus, "Lord, I am sinful, but You can make me clean." Then He says, "I forgive you; you are clean." He washes our sins away by forgiving them, and helps us to live a new kind of life.

Let's talk about this: What kind of trouble did the man in the story have? What did he do when Jesus came to his city? What did he say to Jesus? What did Jesus say to the leper? What happened to the man's sickness? What kind of sickness do we all have? What can Jesus do for us? How do we know that He is willing to help us?

Bible reading for older children and grownups: Mark 1:40-45.

Let us ask Jesus for help: Dear Lord Jesus, we all have the sickness of sin, but You can make us clean. Please take away all our sins so that someday we may be with You and all of God's family in heaven. Amen.

*Whatever you want people to do to you,
do that to them.* Matthew 7:12

How to Treat Others

"You know what I wish?" said Betty to her mother. "I wish somebody would give me a whole pocketful of nickels." She liked chocolate candy bars, and she knew that they cost a nickel apiece at the store.

"Do you know the Bible verse which is called the Golden Rule?" asked Betty's mother. "It says something about 'Whatever you want.'"

Betty knew the verse. She said, "Whatever you want people to do to you, do that to them."

The mother said, "Well, if you want people to give you a pocketful of nickels, what are you supposed to do?"

"Give them the same — but, Mother, how could I?" asked Betty.

"If you couldn't give a pocketful, maybe you shouldn't want others to give you that much," said her mother. "But how about just one nickel? If you had no nickel and you wanted some candy, would you be happy if somebody gave you one nickel?"

"Oh, sure," said Betty.

"Well," said her mother, "the next time you have a nickel and Jean Brown is around, give it to her. She never has any. That will make her happy."

And that's just what Betty did.

Let's talk about this: For what did Betty wish? What did the Bible verse say about wishing? Why would it be wrong to want someone to give us his only bicycle? Because we want people to be nice to us, how are we to treat them? Do we

151

always follow this rule? Let us remember that Jesus wants us to do so.

Older children and grownups may now read: Luke 6:30-35.

Let us ask Jesus to help us: Dear Jesus, we often want other people to do things for us, but we are not willing to do these things for others. Please forgive us for being so selfish, and help us to think about what will make other people happy. We ask this as Your dear children. Amen.

There is forgiveness with God. Psalm 130:4

Where to Get Forgiveness

Once there was a teacher who kept a little black book. In it he put a mark every time he saw one of the children doing something wrong. Some of the boys and girls had many marks in his book. At the end of the week, those who had marks were punished.

If God would keep a book like that and would give us a mark every time we did something wrong, how many marks do you think we would have? So many we could not count them. And in a way God does keep a book like that, because He sees and remembers everything. The Bible calls God's memory a "book."

How can we get rid of the marks against us? There is only one way. The Bible says, "There is forgiveness with God."

152

It is as if all our sins filled a big blackboard with marks. But God is willing to take an eraser and wipe off all the marks behind our name. Then where will the marks be? They will be gone. They won't be anywhere any more.

There is forgiveness with God. There is plenty of forgiveness for all our sins, enough for everybody. Isn't that wonderful? Jesus paid for all the sins of everybody in the whole world. He did this by suffering and dying for us on a cross. That is why there is forgiveness with God for every sin in the whole world.

Many people think they have done things that cannot be forgiven. But it isn't true. Judas sold Jesus. Could Judas have gotten forgiveness? Yes, he could have. Pilate told the soldiers to nail Jesus to the cross. Was Jesus willing to forgive Pilate? Yes, He was.

No matter what it is, there is no sin that cannot be forgiven. There are only sins that *will* not be forgiven because people don't *want* God to forgive them. But we want our sins forgiven, and we are glad that "there is forgiveness with God."

Let's talk about forgiveness: What did one teacher do? If God would do that, how many marks would we have? What does God do with our marks? For how many sins is there forgiveness with God? Are any sins too bad to be forgiven? Why are we glad that God forgives every sin? Why is God willing to forgive all sins?

Bible reading for older children and grownups: Psalm 130:1-8.

Let us pray for forgiveness: Dear Father in heaven, we believe what You have told us, that You are willing to forgive all sins. That is why we can be happy even though we have many marks against us. We love You for letting Jesus suffer and die for us. Please help us to do only what is right and good, for Jesus' sake. Amen.

153

The Soft Answer

"Get out of here," said Bob to his sister Ella, "you're an old cow."

"That's right," said Ella; "moo, moo!" She tried to moo like a cow. Bob laughed, and the quarrel stopped.

Young as she was, Ella had noticed that when somebody is angry at you and says mean words, it never makes things better to shout back a hot answer. Usually a quarrel starts. So Ella just smiled and said something nice or funny.

"A soft answer turns away anger," says God in the Bible. Wars have been started because leaders have said angry words instead of soft words.

At one time the people of Israel went to fight against two of their tribes. Those two tribes had built a large altar by the Jordan River like the altar in the tent church. The other people of Israel thought the two tribes were starting their own religion.

But before fighting, the leaders of Israel sent some men to ask the two tribes why they were not loving the Lord any more. The two tribes answered in a very kind way that they were not starting to love a different god. They were only trying to help their children to remember the true God. That was a soft answer. It stopped the war.

Remember: A soft answer turns away anger. Try it. The Bible says: "Christ suffered for us and left us an example that you should follow His steps. . . . He was cursed, but He did not curse back; He suffered, but He did not threaten."

Let's talk about this: How do we usually answer when somebody yells at us? If the two tribes had answered, "Mind

154

your own business," what might have happened? How did Jesus answer His enemies when He was hanging on the cross? How would you answer if someone said, "You're a liar"? Why is a soft answer better than a hard answer? Let's say the Bible verse together.

Bible reading for older children and grownups: 1 Peter 2:21-25.

Let us pray together: Dear Father in heaven, please forgive us for often becoming angry. Help us to be kind and gentle, like Jesus, who did not give back angry words when people made fun of Him. In His name we pray for a heart that is willing to give soft answers. Amen.

The blood of Jesus Christ, God's Son, cleanses us from all sin. 1 John 1:7

More Wonderful Than Soap

"Look, Mother, I got my hand in some tar, and I can't wash it off," said Clarence.

"I think I know what will take it off," said his mother. She went to the cupboard above the sink and took down a can of greasy soap. "Rub this on your hand," she said, "and then dry it off on a paper towel. Don't use any water."

Clarence did that, and sure enough, his hand became clean, cleaner than it had been for a long time.

"That sure is good stuff," said Clarence.

"Yes, but it can't clean your heart," said his mother. "There's only one thing that cleans a person's heart."

"What's that?" asked Clarence.

"The blood of Jesus," said his mother. "Remember the Bible verse which says, 'The blood of Jesus Christ cleans us from all sin' "?

"Why does our heart need cleaning?" asked Clarence. "It's inside our body, and dirt can't touch it."

"Well, you see," said his mother, "when the Bible talks about our heart, it means what we think and feel. Our thinking and feeling are sometimes called our soul or our spirit."

"Oh," said Clarence. "Sometimes I think wrong things, or my feelings aren't right; that's because my heart isn't clean and pure."

"That's right," said his mother. "The Bible tells us that everyone's heart is black with sin. Sin is like dirt or tar that won't come off by rubbing it with water or by covering it up. But when we ask Jesus to take away our sins, then 'the blood of Jesus Christ, God's Son, cleans our hearts.' That's because He paid for all sins when He died on a cross."

Let's talk about this: What does the Bible mean when it says that everyone's heart is dirty? Is it really our heart or our thinking that is dirty? What washes away our sins and cleans our hearts? Can you say the Bible verse? How did Jesus give His blood for the sins of all people? When does His blood wash our hearts clean?

Older children and grownups may now read: 1 John 1:5-10.

Let us pray to Jesus together: Thank You, dear Lord Jesus, for dying for us on the cross. Forgive what we have done wrong again today. We are glad that You wash away all our sins as soon as we do them. Please keep our hearts clean by keeping us from sin. Amen.

*The hearing ear and the seeing eye, the Lord
has made them both.* Proverbs 20:12

Two Reasons for Being Happy

"I'd rather lose my eyes than my ears," said Ralph. "As long as I had my ears, I could hear people talk. They could tell me everything, and I could talk back to them. I could also listen to my radio."

"I'd rather lose my ears than my eyes," said Joan. "As long as I could see people or flowers or my dog or what's around me, I'd be happy."

Ralph and Joan talked like that for quite a while. Both said that it's good to have eyes and good to have ears. And those who have both have two good reasons for being thankful to God.

The Bible reminds us that "the hearing ear and the seeing eye, the Lord has made them both." Only the eyes which God makes are seeing eyes, and only the ears which God makes are hearing ears. People can make glass eyes, but these cannot see. And people can make false ears, but these cannot hear.

A blind man would be very thankful if he could see. A deaf man would be happy if he could hear. If we can hear and see, let us thank God and be happy, for "the hearing ear and the seeing eye, the Lord has made them both."

Let's talk about this: Which do you think would be better, to have eyes or to have ears, if you couldn't have both? Why do you think so? What's the difference between a glass eye and the eye God makes? What kind of ear can no man make? How would a blind man feel if suddenly he could see? What reasons do we have for being thankful and happy?

157

Bible reading for older children and grownups: Proverbs 20:11-15.

Let us pray together: For our wonderful eyes we thank You, dear God. We thank You also for ears which can hear. Please forgive us if we have used our eyes and ears for sinful seeing and hearing. Help us to use them only for what is good. We ask this in Jesus' name. Amen.

Honor your father and your
mother. Ephesians 6:2

The Captains of Our Home

"We want Richard to be our captain," said the boys on the ball team. So Richard said he would be their captain. But when he told Pete to play first base, Pete said, "Not me; I want to bat." Mike said, "I won't play third base. I want to be the pitcher."

Nobody wanted to do what Richard asked them to do. They said he was their captain, but they did not honor him as their captain. So how could he be their captain? Richard soon quit trying to be the captain.

God gives a daddy and a mother to children. We call them parents. God wants parents to be the captains of their families. And God has said, "Honor your father and your mother." He wants children to obey them, love them, and help them.

How can parents do their best for their children if their children do not honor them? How can they teach their children if the children won't listen to them? How can a home be a happy place when children do as they please and don't obey their parents?

158

God wants children to obey their parents. But that's not all. That isn't even the main thing. "Honor them," says God. To honor parents means to love and obey them because they are the parents. It means letting them decide how things should be, like the captain of a team. Children who obey only when they have to, do not honor their parents. Those who honor their father and mother gladly do what their parents want.

God also expects parents to love their children and to take good care of them. He wants fathers and mothers to see to it that their children grow up as His children. That is why God wants parents to teach their children about Jesus, their Savior, and to show them how to please Jesus every day.

Let's talk about this: Why did Richard quit being the captain of the ball team? Who are the captains in our home? Who made them the captains? Why should we listen to them? What does it mean to honor your father and mother? Do you think that most children honor their father and mother? Which homes are happy homes: those in which father and mother are honored or those in which the children try to be the captains?

Bible reading for older children and adults: Ephesians 6:1-4.

Let us pray together: Dear Father in heaven, we know that we have not always honored our father and mother as we should have. Please forgive us for Jesus' sake. Help all of us in this house to do Your will because we love Jesus, our Savior, who died for us. Amen.

The day is God's; the night also. Psalm 74:16

Why God Made the Night

Karen was afraid of the dark. She liked to go outside and play in the daytime. But when it was dark, she wouldn't go outside unless her mother was real close. She was even afraid to go into her bedroom without a light.

One night she prayed, "Thank You, God, for the sunshine and for the daytime." But she didn't thank Him for the night. Her mother said, "Why don't you thank God also for the night?" Karen answered, "I don't like the night."

Karen's mother said, "Would you like to learn another Bible verse? It tells us who makes the night." Karen nodded her head, so Mother folded Karen's little hands in hers. "The day is God's; the night also," she said. Karen repeated the words, "The day is God's; the night also."

160

"Does the night really belong to God? Does God make it?" asked Karen.

"Yes," answered her mother, "don't you remember how God made the sun to shine by day and the moon to shine at night? God makes it dark so that people won't work all the time. Even most animals and plants rest at night. When it is dark, it is easier to sleep. God made the night so that you could sleep well."

Karen said, "I'll try going to sleep without a light tonight, Mother." So Mother turned off the light, and soon Karen was asleep.

Let's talk about this: Why didn't Karen like the night? Why didn't she thank God for it? What Bible words did her mother tell her? What is one reason why God made the nighttime dark? Why was Karen willing to go to sleep without a light?

Bible reading for older children and grownups: Psalm 74:12-17.

Let us thank God for nighttime as well as the daytime: Dear Father in heaven, we are glad that You give us sunshine and light, but we thank You also for the night. Give us all a quiet sleep so that we will feel rested in the morning. We ask this in Jesus' name. Amen.

Jesus said, God is a spirit. John 4:24

What Does God Look Like?

A painter wanted to show God making the world. So he painted a big man with great big cheeks, blowing some wind. That was supposed to be God sending the wind to separate the water from the land.

Another painter who wanted to paint God made a lot of light come from some clouds. He didn't show God at all. The bright light showed that God was near.

Then there was a third painter. He made God look like an old man with white hair who was kind and good. This was supposed to be a picture of our Father in heaven.

God is a spirit. In some ways a spirit is like a voice out of the radio. You don't get a chair for that voice to sit on, do you? You don't give it something to eat, do you? You can't see it, can you? But the voice is really there just the same.

When Jesus said, "God is a spirit," He meant that God has no body. So you can't see a spirit. But God is everywhere at all times.

Of course, people saw God when Jesus lived on earth, because Jesus is God. But now no one knows what God looks like. We only know that He is great and powerful and very kind and good.

So, which painter was most nearly right? Perhaps it was the one who made the light shine out of the clouds. Jesus said, "People who worship God must worship Him in spirit and in truth." This means that we must believe what the Bible tells us about Him and really love Him.

Let's think about this: Can you think of something that is real even though you can't see it? Can you see the air

162

around you or the wind? Can you draw a picture of love? Why can't we see God even though He is always with us and near us? What did Jesus mean when He said, "God is a spirit"? Remember that God wants to live in our hearts.

Bible reading for older children and grownups: John 4:19-26.

Let's talk to God together: Dear God, we are glad that You are kind and good, and we want You to live in our hearts. Help us to love Jesus. Please make us more like Him by giving us the Holy Spirit. We ask this in Jesus' name. Amen.

Remember the wonderful works which God has done. Psalm 105:5

Wonderful Things God Can Do

Two teams were playing an exciting game at the ball park.

"My daddy is going to hit a home run," said little Billy. He knew that his daddy could. How did he know? His daddy had done it before. He had done it in the last game. That's what Billy remembered. So he believed his daddy could do it again.

Billy thought his daddy was about the strongest man in the whole world. Billy remembered what his daddy could do. He was glad his daddy was strong.

Our Father in heaven is much stronger than any father on earth. He is almighty. That means, He can really do anything He wants to do. He has done many wonderful things. The Bible tells us of some of the great works which He did long ago.

When a poor widow had only a little flour left to eat, God made it last a long time. When a wicked king put three of God's children into a fiery furnace, they didn't burn one bit. God helped the boy David win a fight with a giant. The Old Testament is full of stories of wonderful works which God has done.

While God's Son, Jesus, was on earth, He did many wonderful works which showed His power. He healed the sick people who came to Him. He fed many people with just a little bread. He stopped a big storm on a lake. He even made dead people live again.

The Bible says, "Remember the wonderful works which God has done." If we will remember them, then we will know that God can do them again. He can do wonderful things for us. And He will.

Let's talk about this: Why did Billy think his daddy could hit a home run? What are some of the wonderful things our Father in heaven has done? Why should we remember the wonderful works which God has done? The most wonderful thing God did was to send His Son Jesus to die for us. Why did God do this?

Bible reading for older children and grownups: Psalm 105:1-5.

Let us pray together: You loved us so very much, dear God, when You sent Jesus to save us. Please help us to remember all that You have done. Then we will not be afraid the next time we are in trouble, because we will know that You love us. We praise and thank You for all Your wonderful works, especially for sending Your Son Jesus to save us. Amen.

Wash me ... and cleanse me
from my sins. Ps. 51:2

How God Forgives Sins

"What happens to our sins when God forgives them?" little Jimmy asked his mother. "Where do they go?"

"Tell me," said his mother, "where did all the marks go which you wrote on your slate yesterday?"

"I just washed them away, Mother," said Jimmy. "They aren't anywhere; they are gone."

"That's what happens to our sins when God forgives them, Jimmy," said his mother. "They are washed away. They aren't anywhere; they are gone."

Isn't God's forgiveness wonderful? Our angry words, our lies, all the times we disobey or are mean — where are all these sins? When we ask God to forgive us for Jesus' sake, they are washed away. They are forgiven. God says He will not even remember them.

God forgives us because Jesus paid for all sins. Jesus paid for them by dying on the cross for us. Can we ever thank Jesus enough for that? One way of thanking Him is by not wanting to sin any more.

Let's talk about this: Where do our sins go when they are forgiven? Who forgives them? Why is the heavenly Father willing to forgive all our sins? In the Lord's Prayer, how do we ask for forgiveness of sins? What are some of the sins that we want God to wash away? Remember, every day our Father in heaven is willing to wash away all our sins for Jesus' sake. He is willing because Jesus paid for all sins on the cross.

Older children and grownups may now read: Psalm 51:1-3, 9-11.

Let us ask God to wash away all our sins: Dear Father in heaven, we are ashamed of our many sins, and we are sorry. Please wash us and make us whiter than snow, for Jesus' sake. Amen.

You should not hate your brother. Leviticus 19:17

Don't Lose Your Temper

Billy could get angry so easily! When some little thing did not suit him, he would stamp his feet. He would scream. He would even roll on the ground.

As Billy grew older, he still had a bad temper. If people didn't do what he wanted, he would say mean things or pout and plan ways of hurting people.

Billy noticed that his little brother John was not that way. His mother said, "Billy, why can't you be more gentle and kind? I'm glad Johnny doesn't get so angry." That made Billy angry at his brother.

When a person is angry with someone for a long time, we call that "hate." Long ago Cain hated his brother Abel. One day they were out in a field. Cain became so angry that he killed his brother. This all started when Cain began to hate.

God tells us in the Bible, "You should not hate your brother." God wants us to love, not to hate. "God is Love," says the Bible. "Whoever hates is a murderer, and no murderer has God in his heart."

God loved the whole world very much. He had His Son Jesus die for all people. Jesus was willing to suffer and die because He loved us. Jesus said, "A new commandment I give to you: Love one another as I have loved you. By this shall all men know that you are My disciples, if you love one another."

Let's talk about this: Why is it a sin to hate anyone? Why did Billy often become angry? Who do you think was happier, Billy or Johnny? What happened when Cain became angry? When we feel ourselves getting angry, what might be a good thing for us to do?

Older children and grownups may now read: Genesis 4:3-8.

Let us pray together: Heavenly Father, please forgive us for getting angry so easily. Keep us from losing our temper and hating our brother or friend or neighbor. Make us loving and kind, more like Jesus, every day. Amen.

*Jesus said, She has done
what she could.* Mark 14:8

Doing the Best You Can

Jesus was having dinner in the house of Simon, who had been a leper. Simon had invited Jesus and His disciples to his house for dinner. It was just a few days before Jesus died on a cross.

While they were eating, Mary came into the room. She was carrying a little jar of very expensive perfume. She wanted to show Jesus how much she loved Him. So she stood next to Jesus and poured the perfume on His head. Soon the perfume could be smelled all over the house.

It was then that Judas scolded Mary. "Why has this perfume been wasted?" he asked. "It might have been sold, and the money could have been given to the poor." Some of the other disciples also thought so.

Mary thought this was the best way she could show her love to Jesus, who would soon die for her. When Jesus heard His disciples scold Mary, He said to them: "Let her alone. Why do you scold her? She has done a good thing to Me. She has done the best she could think of." Jesus didn't want Mary to feel ashamed of what she had done. He appreciated her gift of love.

Aren't you glad that Jesus looks at the reasons *why* people do things? Sometimes we try to do something good, and it seems to turn out all wrong. But when Jesus knows that we have done something out of love for Him, He is pleased. He will say, "It was a good work," no matter what we did. But let us do the very best we can so that Jesus will also say of us, "You have done what you could."

Let's think about this: What did Mary do at the home of Simon, the leper? Why did some of the men scold her? What did Jesus say to them? Why was Jesus pleased with what Mary had done? What does Jesus think of the things we do out of love for Him? Why ought we to do what we can?

Older children and grownups may now read the story in the Bible: Mark 14:3-9.

Let us pray together: We are glad that You were so kind to Mary, dear Jesus, and that You look not so much at *what* we do but at the reason *why* we do it. Be pleased with whatever we may do for You, and help us to give You our very best. We love You, as did Mary. Amen.

168

Pray for your enemies. Matthew 5:44

What You Can Do to Get Even

Rocks were flying. People were throwing them at a man for saying that he believed in Jesus. The rocks hit his chest; they hit his face and his back. Pretty soon he would be dead.

Just before he died, he prayed. Did he ask God to punish his enemies? No! He said, "Lord, please do not punish them for this sin." When he had said that, Stephen died.

Stephen prayed for his enemies. Where had he learned to do that? He learned it from Jesus. When the soldiers were nailing Jesus to a cross, Jesus did not hate them. No, He prayed for them and said, "Heavenly Father, forgive them, because they do not know what they are doing."

That's the way Jesus told us to treat people who aren't nice to us. Can you remember the words? "Do good to them that hate you, and pray for those who are mean to you and want to hurt you." The next time you feel angry at somebody, try doing what Jesus did: pray for him.

Let's talk about this: What happened to Stephen, one of the friends of Jesus? How did he pray for his enemies? From whom did he learn this? When did Jesus pray for those who were mean to Him? Can a person hate someone and pray for him at the same time? Why is it hard to pray for someone we don't like? Who will help us to pray for our enemies?

Older children and grownups may now read: Acts 7:54-60.

Let us pray together: Dear Jesus, we know how much You love and forgive us even though we do many wrong things. Help us to forgive and to pray for those who do wrong things to us. Amen.

169

Jesus said, My words will not pass away. Matthew 24:35

Jesus Will Keep His Word

"Yes," said the carpenter, "I will build you a house." But he fell from a roof and died. So his words passed away. He did not build the house he had said he would build. He could not keep his word.

"Yes," said the salesman, "I will sell you a car which will give you no trouble." But his words were no good. A few months later the car gave the man much trouble. The salesman's promise was no good.

"I won't let you go through this door," said a bully at school. The teacher heard him and said, "You get away from there and let the girl through." So the boy's words passed away. They did not come true.

Many people's words pass away. Many of our words pass away. But Jesus said, "My words will not pass away." The words of Jesus will come true, no matter what happens.

When Jesus says, "I will forgive you your sins," we can depend on it. He will do so. When Jesus says, "I am with you," we can depend on that. It's really true. When Jesus says, "I will give you eternal life in heaven," we can depend on that.

Jesus will keep all of His promises. That is what He meant when He said, "My words will not pass away." Isn't that good news?

Let's talk about this: Why could the carpenter not keep his words? What happened to the salesman's promise? Whose words were stronger than the bully's words? Whose words will never pass away? Why are we glad about that? Can you say our Bible verse for today?

Older children and grownups may now read: John 10:27-30.

Let us pray together: Lord Jesus, how happy we are to know that Your words will never pass away, especially Your wonderful promises. Help us to keep them in our minds and hearts so that we may never lose them by forgetting them. Thank you for promising that You will always keep Your word. Amen.

Love is of God. 1 John 4:7

Where Love Comes From

"Joan is very good about taking care of little Judy. They seem to love each other very much," said Mr. Winter to Joan's father. Mr. Winter had come over to Joan's house to speak to her father about some business. Little Judy had come along.

"God wants us to love each other, doesn't He?" said Joan after Mr. Winter and Judy had gone home.

"Yes, Joan," said her father. "I know a Bible verse which says just that."

171

"Tell it to me, Daddy," said Joan. So her father told her the words, "Love one another, for love is of God."

Joan repeated the verse. She wanted to remember it. "Love one another, for love is of God," she said. Already she knew the words, but she said them a few more times so she wouldn't forget them.

"All love comes from God," said her father. "And anybody who doesn't love, doesn't know how God thinks and feels. But those who love have God in their hearts, and they know what God is like. You know how much God loves us, don't you, Joan?"

"Yes," said Joan, "God showed how much He loves us by sending Jesus to die for us. Jesus paid for our sins so that we could have forgiveness and a wonderful life with God. My Sunday school teacher told me that."

The Bible says, "If God so loved us, we ought also to love one another." Those who have Jesus in their hearts will love one another, because He is full of love. "Let us love one another, for love is of God."

Let's talk about God's kind of love: How did God show His love to us? Why was Jesus willing to die for us? Whom did Jesus love? Whom should we love? Why will we love other people if Jesus is in our hearts? Can Jesus stay in the hearts of those who do not love other people?

Bible reading for older children and grownups: 1 John 4:7-11.

Let us pray for a more loving heart: Dear Jesus, our God and Lord, we know how full of love You are, and we are glad that You give love to the world. We wish everybody would love everyone else; how wonderful that would be! Please live in our hearts, Lord Jesus, so that we will love one another. Amen.

He saved others; Himself He
cannot save. Matthew 27:42

Why Jesus Died

When Jesus was hanging on the cross, the people who hated Him did not feel sorry for Him. They made fun of Him and dared Him to come down from the cross. But one thing that they said was true, even though they were laughing at Jesus when they said it. "He saved others," they said; "Himself He cannot save."

That's exactly why Jesus stayed on the cross instead of coming down. He could have saved Himself. But if He had saved Himself, then He would not have saved us. To save others, He could not save Himself. To save you and me from God's punishment of sin, He had to stay on the cross and be punished for us.

It's a little like this: Once there was a great flood, and a family was sitting on the roof of a house, waiting to be rescued. A man came by with a little boat. There was room in the boat for all but one. If everyone tried to get in, the boat would go down. "Save my family, and leave me here," said the father. To save the others, he couldn't save himself.

There is a story about a hen that sat on her nest in some dry grass. Ten baby chicks were under her wings. The grass was burning all around her. The hen could have flown away and saved herself, but then her baby chicks would have burned. So the hen stayed on the nest. Her feathers burned, and she died, but under her were the chicks, safe and alive. She had saved them. That's why she could not save herself.

The Bible says that our Lord Jesus died for us in order to save us. That's why it was true what His enemies said in fun, "He saved others; Himself He cannot save."

173

Let's talk about this: Who made fun of Jesus hanging on the cross? What did they say? In what way was it true? In what way was it not true? Why could the father in the flood not save himself? Why couldn't the hen save herself? What do you think we owe Jesus for saving us instead of saving Himself?

Bible reading for older children and grownups: Matthew 27:38-44.

Let us pray together: Thank You, dear Lord Jesus, for staying on the cross. Thank You for saving us when You could have saved Yourself. Make us willing to give up our lives so that others may learn what You have done for them. Amen.

God so loved the world that He gave His only Son. John 3:16

Does God Love Bad People?

"You aren't supposed to do that," said Ben to his little brother Mike. "When you do that, you are naughty, and God doesn't love bad people."

Was Ben right or wrong?

He was very wrong. Everybody does wrong things, and God loves us even when we aren't good. But He does not love the naughty things we do.

The Bible says that God loves the whole world. God loved the whole world so much that He gave them a present. It was the best present He could give. He gave His Son, His only Son, to the world. He did this when He sent Jesus to be everybody's Savior. When God sent His only Son, Jesus, to save all people, He showed how much He loves every person.

174

God gave His Son Jesus to the world; that means, to every person who ever would live in the world. Anyone can have Jesus as his Savior just by wanting Jesus to save him. And the Bible says, "Anyone who believes in Jesus will receive a life that never ends in heaven," a life with God.

Now, can't you see why Ben was wrong? God wants even the bad people and the naughty children in heaven.

Let's talk about God's love: What did Ben say about God? Why was Ben wrong? How did God show that He loves the world? Who all is meant by the world? How can anyone have Jesus as his Savior? What does Jesus do with all sins? What does Jesus promise to all who want Him to save them?

Older children and grownups may now read: John 3:14-17.

Let us pray together: Thank You, dear God, for loving the whole world and all people in it even though they all do wrong. Please forgive us when we are naughty, and help us to live the way You want us to live. We want You to be our Savior, and we want to be God's children. Amen.

Christ died for our sins. 1 Corinthians 15:3

What He Did Counts for Me

Little Lester was crying softly. He was in his pajamas, ready for bed, and was looking at a picture of Jesus nailed to a cross.

"What are you crying about?" asked his daddy.

"They put nails through His hands and feet," said Lester as he brought the book to daddy. "He let them do it to Him so that it would count for us."

"Yes," said his daddy, "Jesus loved us that much. He was

175

willing to be hurt so that we wouldn't be punished for the naughty things we do."

"Like when I hit Betty?" asked Lester. Betty was his sister.

"Yes, or when you don't listen to your mother."

Lester climbed up on his daddy's lap and hugged him. "I love you real much, Daddy," he said. "But Jesus loved us even more, didn't He?"

"Yes, He did," said Lester's daddy. "He did all the things God wants us to do, and then He died for us. And what He did counts for us. Because of what He did, God forgives us and is willing to have us as His children."

"And that's why we can go to heaven," said Lester. Then he kissed the picture of Jesus and ran off happily to bed.

Let's talk about this: Why was Lester crying? Why did Jesus let people hang Him on a cross? What do we mean when we say, "What Jesus did counts for us"? Why was Lester happy when he went to bed? Let's say the Bible verse together.

Bible reading for older children and grownups: Luke 23:44-49.

Let us thank Jesus in prayer: We thank You, dear Jesus, for all that You did for us so that we could have forgiveness of sins. Help us never to forget how You suffered and died. Make us sorry for sinning, and help us to live holy lives for Your sake. Amen.

Do not give place to the
devil. Ephesians 4:27

How to Keep from Sinning

"Don't stay in the kitchen, Irene," said a mother to her little girl. "As long as you see the cake, you will want to taste it."

Twice Irene had tried to eat some of the cake which her mother wanted for a party that night.

"I don't want to eat the cake. I just want to look at it," said Irene.

"Then let's sit down here and learn a Bible verse," said her mother. "The Bible verse says, 'Do not give place to the devil.'"

"Margie says there is no devil," Irene told her mother.

"Jesus said there is," answered the mother, "and if it weren't so, He would have told us. The devil tries to make us do wrong, but he can't if we don't give him a chance. That's why the Bible says, 'Do not give place to the devil.' Don't let him have any place around you or in you."

Little Irene began to think. "When I stay near the cake, am I giving the devil a place where he can get me to do wrong?" asked Irene.

177

"I'm afraid so, Honey," said her mother.

"Then I'd better go to a place where I don't see the cake," said Irene.

"I'm glad you learn fast," said Irene's mother. "Let's never let the devil stay around us. He's always trying to get people to do wrong. And we don't want to do wrong, do we?" said Irene's mother.

"No," said Irene. "We belong to Jesus."

Let's talk about this: Is it wrong to eat cake? Why was it wrong for Irene to eat her mother's cake? Where did Irene want to stay? Which Bible verse did her mother teach her? What did Irene think she had better do? Why?

Bible reading for older children and grownups: Ephesians 6:10-17.

Let us pray together: Dear God, we are sorry that we have often given a place to the devil. Please forgive every wrong we have ever done. Keep us from letting the devil have even a little place in us and around us. We know that we belong to Jesus, and we want to be like Him. We ask this in Jesus' name. Amen.

The earth is full of the riches
of God. Psalm 104:24

The Riches of God

Mr. Smith was as happy as a little boy when he came home one day. "Mother," he said, "we're rich. Our oil well came in. It's a gusher. We'll never have to work again."

The whole family piled into the car and drove out to the field to see the oil well. "Don't worry," said Mr. Smith to his wife, who stood shaking her head. "I'm going to keep on

178

working just the same. Only now I'll work to help other people who need it."

Billy and Betty watched the oil come up from way down in the earth. "It's just as though God filled the earth with oil for us," said Betty.

"God did fill this hole with oil for us," said their father.

Billy was thinking. In their geography books they had learned about iron and coal and diamonds and many other things lying in the earth, ready for somebody to dig up.

"The earth is full of good things, isn't it?" said Billy.

"That's almost a Bible verse," said his mother. "I know a psalm which says, 'The earth is full of the riches of God.'"

"Mother," said Betty, "there are many good things on top of the earth, too. There are flowers and trees and grass and bushes and hundreds of other things."

"Hey, you didn't mention animals or birds. God made them, too," said Billy.

"That's right," said Mr. Smith, still watching the oil come out of the ground. "The earth is full of the riches of God. That's why the psalm writer said, 'I will sing unto the Lord as long as I live; I will sing praises to my God while I have my being.'"

Let's talk about this: Who put the oil into the earth? What are some other good things that God put into the earth? What showed that Mr. Smith believed in God? What are some of the things God puts on the earth? Can you say the Bible verse which Billy's mother knew?

Older children and grownups may now read: Psalm 65:9-13.

Let us thank God for His many gifts: Dear Lord, You weren't stingy when You made the earth. You made it rich with many gifts for us. We thank You for all these good things. Please help us to use them rightly for ourselves and for the good of others, for Jesus' sake. Amen.

Jesus said, Whoever will do the will of My Father . . .
is My brother and sister and mother. Matthew 12:50

Relatives of Jesus

Who do you suppose came to see Jesus one day when He was preaching to a large group of people? It was His mother and His brothers. Long ago cousins were also called "brothers," so maybe His "brothers" were cousins.

These relatives of Jesus wanted to talk to Him. But the crowd was so big that they could not get near Him. Somebody came and told Jesus, "Your mother and Your brothers are standing back there behind all the people. They want to talk with You."

Did Jesus stop teaching and run to see His mother? No, He did not. What He was doing was more important than talking to His mother. He was teaching the Word of God.

And Jesus wanted the people to know how important the Word of God is. So He said, "Who is My mother? Who are My brothers?" Then He pointed to His disciples and said, "Look, there are My mother and My brothers. Whoever will do the will of My Father . . . is My brother and sister and mother."

How many people could be brothers and sisters and mothers of Jesus that way? Why, all of us could. The first thing God wants us to do is to believe in Jesus. And when we believe in Jesus and love Him, we gladly obey the heavenly Father. Jesus, our Savior, makes us God's children, and then we are sisters and brothers of Jesus.

Let's talk about this: Who came to see Jesus one day? What was Jesus doing? Why didn't He quit preaching and talk to His relatives? Who did He say were His brothers and sisters and mother? How can we be His brothers and sisters?

Older children and grownups may now read: Matthew 12:46-50.

Let us pray together: Dear Jesus, please let us be Your brother or sister. Make us glad to do Your heavenly Father's will. Make us children of God by washing away all of our sins, and help us to obey God's Word in all things. Amen.

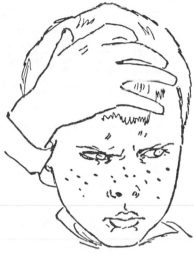

It is good for me that I have been in trouble. Psalm 119:71

Some Troubles Are Good

"They caught Jimmy stealing," said Buddy. "I'm glad. That's good for him."

It wasn't right for Buddy to talk like that, but in one way Buddy was right. It was good for Jimmy that he got caught. If he hadn't been caught, he might have kept on stealing, and that would have been much worse.

But now the police took Jimmy to the station. There a police officer talked to him a long while. At last he said, "If

181

you will let the pastor of your church help you, I will give you another chance. Every day you must phone or see the pastor and tell him where you are and what you are doing. And you must go to Sunday school."

Jimmy promised that he would report to his pastor every day, that he would never steal again, and that he would go to Sunday school.

Soon Jimmy got to be good friends with his pastor. The pastor reminded Jimmy every day that he was one of God's children. "You belong to God," said the pastor. "Jesus suffered and died on a cross for your sins so that you could have them all forgiven. He's willing to keep on forgiving you if you will let Him. But God's children, who love Jesus, do not want to steal. If you want to keep on stealing, you can't be one of God's children."

"I'm sorry I did wrong," said Jimmy. "I forgot what I learned at Sunday school. But I won't miss any more. And I'm asking Jesus to help me every day so that I won't steal any more." All this happened because Jimmy got into trouble. It was good for Jim that he had been in trouble.

Let's talk about this: How did Jimmy get into trouble? What did Jimmy promise the police officer? What good came out of his trouble? Can we remember any trouble we may have had in our family? Did any good come out of it? What did the psalm writer say because he learned more about God through his troubles? (Say the memory verse.)

Bible reading for older children and grownups: Psalm 119:71-77.

Let us pray: Dear loving Lord Jesus, help us never to forget that You have made us God's dear children. Teach us to live as God's children, even if You must let troubles come to us in order to do so. Thank You for always being willing to forgive us. Amen.

182

Two Places Where God Lives

"Wish I could be Mr. Smith," said Tommy one day to Sally.

"Why?" asked Sally. Sally lived next door.

"In summer, when it's nice here, he lives here. In winter, when it's cold here, he lives in Florida. He lives in two places."

"I know somebody else who lives in two places," said Sally.

"Who?" asked Tom.

"God. He lives up in heaven, and He lives in my heart."

"He does?" said Tom. "How do you know that?"

"My mother read that in the Bible this morning," said Sally. Just then Sally's mother came out and sat down on the steps with her Bible. Tom sat on one side of her and Sally on the other.

"Let me read what God says in the Bible," she said. "God says, 'I live in the high and holy place; with him also who is of a . . . humble spirit.'"

"High and holy place is heaven, isn't it?" asked Sally.

"Yes," answered her mother, "and the person who has a humble spirit is one who knows he isn't good enough to live with God. God is willing to live with him if he wants God's forgiveness."

"Will God live with me, too?" asked Tom.

"Certainly," said Sally's mother. "God will be glad to live with you. He will forgive your sins for Jesus' sake because Jesus died for you on a cross. God lives in your heart right now because you love Jesus. That's why you are one of God's children."

Sally was glad to hear this.

Let's talk about this first: God is everywhere, but in which two places does this Bible verse say God lives? Where is the high and holy place? What kind of persons have a humble spirit? Why is God willing to live with people who are sorry they have sinned and are not proud? Let's say the Bible verse together several times. Now let us pray for a humble spirit so that God will live in our hearts and in our home.

Older children and grownups may now read: Isaiah 57:19-21.

A prayer for a humble spirit: Dear Lord, we know that we are not holy, like You. We know that we are not good enough to have You live with us. But we are glad You are willing to live in us anyway. Please forgive us our sins, and keep us all as Your dear children, for Jesus' sake. Amen.

*God says, I am the First, and I am the Last,
and beside Me there is no God.* Isaiah 44:6

Make-Believe Gods

Irene wanted a little sister. But God did not give her a little sister. So Irene put some long dresses on her biggest doll and said, "This is my sister Ruth." But she was making believe. Only God can make a sister. Nobody can make a sister out of a doll.

Many years before Jesus lived on earth, the people of Israel loved the true God and were His children. But most other people made their own gods. They made a man or an animal out of a stone or a tree and called these statues their gods.

These gods were make-believe gods. But the people thought they were real. They even prayed to them. Irene knew better than that. She couldn't even make a sister, so how could anyone make a god?

Today many people still make their own gods. In India and Africa and Japan and many other countries children pray to gods who really aren't gods. In our country we don't have such gods. But whatever we love most is really our god. What are some of the things people love very much? Money, houses, cars, TV shows, candy, and many other things. These are our gods if we love them more than we love God.

Do we love Jesus and our heavenly Father and the Holy Spirit more than anything else? They are the one and only real God. That's why God ought always to be first and last and most important in our hearts.

Let's talk about this: How did Irene make a sister? What kind of gods do some people make? A god is something we love more than anything else. What are some of the things people love more than God in our country? Who is the only real God who ever was or ever will be? Whom ought we to love more than anybody or anything else?

Older children and grownups may now read: Isaiah 44:1-6.

Let us pray together: We are glad, dear God, that You are our God and that You always will be. We want nobody else but You for our God. Please forgive us for not always loving You more than anything else. Please help us to trust in You above all things. We ask this in Jesus' name. Amen.

*Create in me a clean heart,
O God.* Psalm 51:10

How to Get Clean on the Inside

King David was feeling very bad. He had done a great sin. He had taken the pretty wife of one of his soldiers. Then he had gotten rid of the soldier by putting him in the front of a battle. There the soldier was killed, as David had hoped.

For a while David made believe he had done no wrong. He would not even tell God he was sorry.

But God sent the prophet Nathan to David. The prophet said: "God has been very good to you. Why have you done this great sin? You killed Uriah and have taken his wife to be your wife. Very much trouble will now come to you out of your own family. And because the enemies of God are making fun about what you have done, your child will die."

Now David knew that God had seen what he had done, and he felt real bad. He said, "I have sinned against God." What could he do? He asked God to take his sins away. "Please feel sorry for me, dear God," he said. Then he made up a poem for others to say to God, too. It is Psalm 51 in the Bible. The Holy Spirit helped him write it.

In that Psalm 51 King David begged God to forgive him his sins. "Create in me a clean heart, O God," he said. He knew that only God could wash away the wrong he had done. For seven days and nights the great king prayed and would not eat.

King David was punished, as the prophet had said he would be. But because he begged God to wash his sins away, God forgave David so that he could still go to heaven.

"Create in me a clean heart, O God." That's a prayer which every one of us needs to say often, because so often we think and say and do what isn't right. Every sin is like dirt in our hearts, and only God can make our hearts clean. He does this when He forgives us all our sins for Jesus' sake.

Let's think this over: What great sin had King David done? What did the prophet Nathan tell him? Which psalm, or poem, did King David write after Nathan had talked to him? For what did David beg in this psalm? What does "create" mean? How does God make a clean heart in people?

Bible reading for older children and grownups: Psalm 51:10-12.

Let us pray for a clean heart: Create in me a clean heart, O God, by washing away all my sins for Jesus' sake. Amen.

*Let not the sun go down
on your anger.* Ephesians 4:26

Smile Before Sundown

Two young friends were working together in a factory. One morning one of them bent down to pick up a hammer. When he straightened up, the back of his head hit a board. His pal laughed because he thought it was funny. That made the other boy very angry. Without thinking, he hit his pal with the hammer. The pal fell down and died. The young man had killed his best friend.

Not all anger is wrong. Even God sometimes gets angry at sin. Remember how angry Jesus was when He chased the money-makers out of the Temple? God wants us to get rid of whatever is wrong; so it is not a sin to get angry over what is not right.

But anger is something that we must watch very carefully. It's so easy to get angry at people and to get angry without a good reason. Whenever we get so angry that we want to hurt people, we do not love them. And remember, God wants us to love even our worst enemies.

Many people stay angry when they get angry. In our Bible verse, Paul tells us not to let the sun go down on our anger. This means, if we do become angry over something, we had better not keep on being angry for more than a day. Anger that keeps on burning inside of us turns into hate, and hate is even more dangerous than anger.

Remember Cain and Abel? Cain was jealous and angry because God was more pleased with Abel than with him. Cain let his anger grow day after day, and soon it turned into hate. At last one day he killed his brother Abel.

So, "let not the sun go down on your anger." Ask Jesus to help you forgive and forget. He will. Jesus never hated anyone.

Let's talk about anger: What did the young man do to his pal? Why did he do it? Why is anger so very dangerous? Why is it wrong to get angry at people? If we are angry day after day, what does our anger get to be? What did Cain's anger lead to? What does St. Paul say in the memory verse?

Bible reading for older children and grownups: Matthew 6:12-15.

Let us pray together: Our Father in heaven, You are very patient and slow to anger. Help us to be slow in getting angry. Make us kind and gentle, like Jesus, and teach us to become angry only at sin, never at people. When we become angry, help us to get over it before the sun goes down. We ask this in Jesus' name. Amen.

We Are Never Alone

Gertrude was crying. The big boys and girls had gone to the river to swim, but Gertrude was too little to go along. So she had to stay home. That's why she was crying.

"I'm all alone," she said to her mother. "Nobody is here to play with me."

"Well, then, why don't you come and help me mix a cake?" said her mother.

Gertrude wiped her tears and went into the kitchen. Mother gave her a little bit of flour to mix with milk and butter and sugar and other things. It was fun. Soon a big smile spread over Gertrude's face.

"I'm not alone now," she said, "not when I'm with you, Mother."

God's children are never alone, not if God is with them. And God is always everywhere. Sometimes we feel all alone and blue, or sick and worried. Sometimes we think that nobody loves us, and then we feel very much alone. But we are never alone. Jesus said, "I am with you always."

So when you feel alone or left out, unhappy, sick, worried, or frightened, talk to Jesus about it. He will be right

189

there with you and will help you and cheer you. Love Him, and soon you will smile again. "Look," He said, "I am with you always." Don't ever forget that.

Let's talk about this: Why did Gertrude cry? Who made Gertrude smile? How? Why are we never alone? Why do we sometimes feel sad and lonesome? To whom can we speak whenever we feel alone? In how many places is Jesus at the same time?

Bible reading for older children and grownups: John 16:28-33.

Let us tell Jesus that we are glad He is always with us: Dear Lord Jesus, we are glad that You are always with us, even when nobody else is near. Help us to remember that You are always with us, that You love us and are always ready to help us. Please forgive us our sins, and keep on loving us. Then we can be happy all the time. Amen.

Jesus said, Learn of Me, for I am lowly
in heart. Matthew 11:29

Our Lord Is Never Proud

One time some soldiers were building a fort and were having a hard time lifting a log into its place. "Heave away! Heave ho!" shouted their leader, who was a corporal. He shouted at them, but he did not help them.

A man on horseback came along, jumped off his horse, and helped the soldiers. Then he turned to the leader and said, "Why didn't you help them?"

"I?" said the man. "I am a corporal!" He was too proud to do such work. He was too proud to help his men.

Do you know what the rider said as he swung on his horse and rode away? He said to the corporal, "The next time you need help on any work you are too proud to do, call George Washington." The corporal almost fainted. Now he knew who the man was. He was the general in charge of all the soldiers.

Do you think that Jesus would have helped the men, or would He have been too proud to help, like the corporal? Jesus wasn't too proud to do anything that needed to be done to help us. He wasn't too proud to become a baby. He wasn't too proud to help His parents. He wasn't too proud to go to school. He wasn't too proud to work.

Even though Jesus is God, He wasn't too proud to suffer and to die for us. He was not ashamed to have poor people as His friends, not even when other people called them sinners. He loves all of us even though He is great and good and we are nothing.

That's something we can learn from Him. "Learn of Me," He said, "for I am . . . lowly in heart." To be lowly means to be humble and not proud. When we love Jesus, He helps us to be humble.

Let's see what we have learned: Who was too proud to help his soldiers? Who wasn't too proud? How did Jesus show that He is not proud? What does Jesus say in our Bible verse? How can we learn to be lowly in heart?

Bible reading for older children and grownups: Matt. 11:28-30.

Let us pray to be kind and helpful, not proud: Dear Jesus, we are glad that You were not too proud to be a baby and a man in order to save us. Thank You for being willing to die for us on a cross. Please make us lowly in heart and kind and helpful as You are. Amen.

191

Jesus prayed, Father, not My will,
but Thine, be done. Luke 22:42

Doing What God Wants

Twelve men were walking down a hill. Over the creek they went and up again to a garden park on the next hill. As they walked, the Leader was very sad. He was thinking of something that was about to happen.

Soon they came to the gate of the park. There the Leader said to eight of the men, "Stay here and wait for Me; I want to go into the park and pray a while." He took three of His best friends along with Him. Farther in the garden the three sat down, and the Leader went away about as far as you can throw a stone. There He kneeled down and talked to His Father in heaven.

"My Father," He prayed, "please don't let Me suffer and die. But if I must in order to save people, then I will. Help Me to do what *You* want, not what *I* want."

Then He came back to His friends. His friends were sleeping. So He went away again to pray. Three times He did this. He knew that soon He would have to suffer and die to pay for our sins. Each time He said He wanted it to happen if His Father in heaven wanted it to happen.

That Leader was our Lord Jesus. Even though He was God's Son, He could feel hurts and pain. He did not like to be hung on a cross. But because His Father wanted Him to save us, He was willing. He loved us that much.

We are very thankful that Jesus was willing to die for us, else we ourselves would have had to suffer for our sins. Let us show that we love Him by doing whatever He wants.

Let's talk about this: Where did Jesus go with His friends one night? Why was He very sad? How often did He pray

192

in the Garden? What did He say to His Father in heaven? Why was Jesus willing to be hurt and killed? What is the best way to show our love and thanks to Jesus?

Bible reading for older children and grownups: Luke 22:39-46.

Let us pray as Jesus prayed: Dear Father in heaven, we know that You love us because You let Your only Son die for us. He loved us enough to do it. Please help us in all our troubles. But do not do what we want, but do whatever You know is best for us. In Jesus' name we pray this. Amen.

Put away lying. Ephesians 4:25

Always Tell the Truth

"Peter stole some money from a store, I think," said Arnold.

"He did?" said Mrs. White. "Then I can't let him run errands for me any more. I better tell Mr. Samson, too, so that he won't give Peter that job in the store."

Arnold felt very sorry. He didn't mean to say what he had said, and he knew that it might not be true. He wanted to

193

say that he didn't really know for sure, but Mrs. White hurried into her house and closed the door.

Through the window Arnold could see Mrs. White talking on the phone. She was probably talking to the storeman, telling him what she had heard about Peter.

What had Arnold done! By telling a lie he had cheated Peter out of two jobs! He had also spoiled the good thoughts people had about Peter. That's how much harm one little lie can do.

Lies hurt the people who tell them, the people who hear them, and the people about whom they are told. They make people think wrong things, and then they do wrong things because of what they think is true.

Sometimes we tell people wrong things just to tease them. Fooling people is not always lying. But we must be careful even in fun. What we say in fun can often do the work of lies.

A real lie is when you are not honest in talking with people and when you try on purpose to make people believe what is not true. God says, "Put away lying." People who lie do not love the way Jesus wants them to love others. You wouldn't want others to tell lies to you or about you, would you?

Let's talk about lies: What did Arnold say about Peter? Was that a little lie or a big one? What harm did it do? What should Arnold have done? Why is it risky to say what isn't so even if you are just teasing? What is a lie? Why doesn't God want us to tell lies?

Bible reading for older children and grownups: Ephesians 4:25-29.

Let us pray together: Dear God, we know that there is no lie in Your whole Bible and that You hate lies. Please forgive us any lies we have spoken, and help us to put away lying, for Jesus' sake. Amen.

194

*God says, Call upon Me in the day
of trouble.* Psalm 50:15

They Didn't Think God Would

One day King Herod put Simon Peter into jail for preaching about Jesus. The king was going to kill Peter. But the Christians in Jerusalem prayed to God to save Peter. The night before Peter was to be killed, God sent one of His angels to help him. The angel opened the door of the jail and let Peter out.

Peter went to the house where the Christians were praying. A girl named Rhoda told them that Peter was knocking at the door. They said, "You must be crazy." They didn't believe that God would really answer their prayers. But Peter kept on knocking. When they opened the door, they were surprised to see Peter.

God says He will help us, too, when we pray to Him. "Call upon Me in the day of trouble," He says, "and I will help you." The name "God" means "good." He is a good God. He loves us, and He wants to help us. He asks us to tell our troubles to Him.

Sometimes people ask God for help, but they don't really think that God can help them. God can do anything He wishes, and He can help us in any kind of trouble.

So call upon God whenever you have trouble, and believe that He will help you. He will.

Let's talk about this: Why were the Christians praying in Jerusalem when Peter was in jail? How can we tell that they did not expect God to answer their prayers? Can you remember a time when God surprised you and answered your prayer? Why don't we always trust that God will answer our prayers? Let's say the Bible verse together.

Older children and grownups may now read: Acts 12:11-17.

Let us pray together: Dear Lord God, we thank You for inviting us to tell You all our troubles. Thank You for answering our prayers even when we do not think You will. Help us to trust that You will always answer our prayers, for we know You will. We ask this in Jesus' name. Amen.

There shall be no more . . .
  crying. Revelation 21:4

What Heaven Is Like

A little boy had an operation on his eyes. His family was waiting for the doctor to take off the bandages. The doctor said, "Either he will see well, or he won't see at all."

One after another the bandages came off. After the last one the boy put his hands to his eyes. "I can't see," he said slowly. "I must be blind."

His mother started to cry when she heard that. But the boy said, "Don't cry, Mother. I can wait until Jesus takes me to heaven. In heaven I will see again."

What a wonderful thing to know. There'll be no trouble in heaven. Nobody will be blind in heaven. Nobody will be crying in heaven, because there will be nothing to cry about.

Heaven is where Jesus wants us all to be. That's why He came to save us. That's why He died for us on a cross. Aren't you glad He did this for all of us?

Let's talk about this: What do you think most boys and girls would say if they found out they were blind? How did knowing about heaven help this boy? Somebody must have told him about heaven. Who do you think did? What other

196

things do people cry about? Will these things be in heaven? How can we get to heaven?

Older children and grownups may now read: Revelation 21:1-4.

Let us thank God for the promise of heaven: Thank You, dear God, for the promise that Your children will be with You in heaven someday. Please help us in all our troubles, and keep us as Your children, for Jesus' sake. Amen.

In the beginning God created the heaven and the earth. Genesis 1:1

God Made Everything

Dolly and her mother were taking the baby out for a walk. They stopped to rest under a big tree.

"Who made this tree, Mother?" asked Dolly.

"Why, Dolly, you know who made this tree," said her mother.

Dolly laughed. "I was just having some fun," she said. "I know that God makes the trees. He made all the trees in all the parks and on all the farms and in all the woods and

197

". . . and . . ." Dolly was almost out of breath from counting trees.

"Not only the trees but also the bushes and the flowers and the corn and the wheat," said her mother.

"And the water and the clouds and the stars and the sun and everything, the whole world," Dolly said, waving both arms in a big circle. "Mother," she said, "when was 'in the beginning'?" She was thinking of the verse, "In the beginning God created the heaven and the earth."

"The beginning was when God made the heaven and the earth," answered her mother. "God never had any beginning. But one day He started making the heaven and the whole earth, and that was 'in the beginning.'"

Dolly was very quiet for the longest time. She was thinking of how God had made so many, many things, big stars and tiny little bugs. She remembered how He had made them all just by saying, "Let there be this and that."

Let's talk about this: When did God make the first trees from which all other trees have come? What is there in the sky that God has made? What do flowers tell us about God? What did God use in making the world? Who alone can make something out of nothing?

Older children and grownups may now read: Genesis 1:11-28.

Let us praise God together: Dear Father Almighty, Maker of heaven and earth, how great, how wise, how good You are! Thank You for having made all things beautiful. Please help us to be the kind of people You want us to be. We ask this in the name of Jesus, our Savior. Amen.

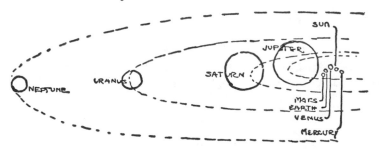

Jesus loved me and gave Himself for me. Galatians 2:20

Why Jesus Gave His Life Away

A boat turned over on a lake. The boy who had been fishing in it went down into the water. A man on the shore saw what happened and dived in after him. He swam to where the boy was and got him out. After the boy was wrapped in a warm blanket and taken home, he was all right.

But the man who had jumped into the water to save the boy caught a very bad cold. It became pneumonia. Soon after that he died.

The boy never forgot the man who had saved him. His parents also were thankful. They did whatever they could to help the man's family. And every year the boy went out to the cemetery and put flowers on the man's grave. He said, "That man saved me and died for me."

Those words sound almost like the words St. Paul said about Jesus. He said, "Jesus loved me and gave Himself for me." But Jesus loved us all much more than anyone else could love us. He became a child. He lived a poor life on earth even though He was God. And He let people hurt Him and nail Him to a cross.

Jesus loved us and gave Himself for us. He gave up His life on purpose so that we could be saved from our sins. We will not want to forget Jesus. All those who believe that Jesus died to save them love Him. Those who love Him also thank Him and work for Him.

Let's think about this: What happened to the boy in the boat? What did a man on the shore do? Why did he die? Why were the boy and his parents thankful? How did Jesus give Himself for us? How many people ought to be thankful

199

to Jesus? Which people are thankful? How can we show our love for Jesus?

Bible reading for older children and grownups: Galatians 2:20.

Let us talk to Jesus in prayer: Dear Jesus, our Savior, we never want to forget You or all the things You have done for us. Help us to show You every day how thankful we are that You gave up Your life for us. Amen.

God's years shall have
   no end. Psalm 102:27

How Old Is God?

"How old is God?" somebody asked a teacher long ago.

The teacher said, "Suppose there were a big mountain of grain a mile high. Suppose that every thousand years a bird came along and picked one grain off that mountain. When that mountain of grain would be eaten up, then one minute of God's life would be gone."

God never started. He always was. He made the world when it started. He made the sun, moon, and stars and the things that you see on earth. He made us. We all started not so very long ago. But God was long before that. God always was. He had no beginning.

Jesus' life never started either, because Jesus is God's Son and is also God like His Father. Jesus started being a baby when He was born in Bethlehem. He became a person like you and me because He wanted to die for our sins. But Jesus was God long, long before that. He had no beginning. He made all things.

And God will never stop living. God's years shall

have no end, says the Bible. God is always the same. He never gets old and dies.

And did you know another thing? We won't ever stop living either if we are God's children. Our bodies may get old and die, but we ourselves will live on and on forever and ever with God in heaven. Jesus said, "Anyone who believes in Me will *never* die." Isn't that wonderful?

Let's talk about this: When did God begin? When will God stop living? Let's say the Bible verse together. Why are God's children happy that God will never die? Whom will Jesus keep alive with Him forever?

Older children and grownups may now read: Psalm 102:25-28.

Let us pray together: Dear Jesus, we are glad that Your years have no end and that You will always be our God. Please be with us every day while we live here on earth, and keep us with You forever in heaven. Amen.

Jesus said, Whatever you will ask the Father in My name, He will give it you. John 16:23

Why We Pray in Jesus' Name

"Mother," said Anne, "why do we often end our prayers 'in Jesus' name'? What does that mean?"

"Let me tell you a story," said her mother. "It may help you to understand what it means to do anything in somebody else's name." This was the story:

A young man named George had a very pretty pony. During the war George had to join the army. In a battle he was hit by some bullets and was badly wounded. His buddy crept out to him and pulled him to a safe place.

But George knew he was dying, so he wrote on a scrap of paper, "I want my father and mother to have everything I own, but I want my buddy to have my pony." Then he signed his name and gave the piece of paper to his friend.

George died, and after a while the buddy was sent home. As soon as he could, he went to see George's parents. While talking to them, he said, "I'd like to have George's pony." George's father said, "I'm sorry; you can't have it. We want George's brother to have it."

Then the soldier showed George's father the slip of paper. The father saw his son's name on the paper. When he read what his son wanted, he was glad to give the soldier the pony.

"I get it," said Anne. "When the soldier asked in his own name, he didn't get the pony, but when he asked in the son's name, then he got it. So when we ask God for anything in our own name, we may not get it, but when we ask in Jesus' name for anything He wants us to have, we are sure to get it. Is that right, Mother?" asked Anne.

"Yes," said Anne's mother. "Jesus said, 'Whatever you will ask the Father in My name, He will give it to you.' Isn't that exciting?"

Let's talk about this: Why didn't the soldier get the pony at first? What made the father willing to give the soldier the pony? Who told us to pray in Jesus' name? Can you tell what it means to pray in Jesus' name?

Bible reading for older children and grownups: John 16:22-27.

Let us pray together: Dear Lord Jesus, how wonderful it is that in Your name we may ask the heavenly Father for anything You want us to have. Thank You for letting us pray to the Father in Your name. Teach us to ask for whatever You want us to have. Then we know that God will give it to us. Amen.

*Make me to go in the path of Your
commandments.* Psalm 119:35

Choosing the Right Path

"Be sure to stay with your leader," said Mr. Lester to his son Fred. Fred and some other boys were getting ready to go on a hike into the mountains.

"I will," Fred promised.

When they came to the first side road, the leader stopped and talked to the boys. "Look," he said, "you will see many paths along the way. Some of them will lead you to the river. Some over the mountain. Some into caves. Be sure to stay on the right path, or you may get lost, and we may never find you. Be sure to stay on the path on which I lead you." They promised to do that, and all got back home safely.

God is like a guide or leader. The path on which He wants us to go is the path of His commandments. His commandments lead us and guide us in the ways we are to follow. God's ways are safe and good. When we do not follow God's commandments, we become lost. We would all be lost forever if Jesus had not saved us.

203

Those who want to be saved by Jesus are glad to follow Him. They know that He will lead them only on the right paths. He will bring them safely to their home in heaven. That is why they say, "Make me to go in the path of Your commandments."

Let's talk about following God's paths: What did the guide tell the boys? Why was it important for them to stay on the right path? What if a boy had said, "I'll go my own way; I know as much as the guide"? On what path does God want us to go? Where do the paths of sin take people? We would all be lost forever if Jesus had not saved us. Why do God's children want to go on the path of God's commandments?

Bible reading for older children and grownups: Psalm 119:33-36.

Let us pray together: Dear Father in heaven, please make us follow the path of Your commandments. We want to follow Jesus, our Lord and Savior. We are glad that He saved us from being lost on wrong paths, and we want to stay on the right path with Him. In His name we pray this. Amen.

It is God who has made us. Psalm 100:3

Our Maker

Billy and his father were in a store. They heard a man with a loud voice talking to some other men. The loud voice said, "Naw, God didn't make me. I don't even believe there is a God. We got here by ourselves."

The other men didn't seem to think so. One of them said, "I don't think even a broom handle gets on a broom by itself. How could your arm get on your shoulder by itself, or how could your two eyes be just in the right place, or how could your mind work the way it does if somebody hadn't planned it?"

Billy and his father said nothing. They just listened a while. On the way home Billy said, "Daddy, that man with the loud voice doesn't know God, does he?"

"No, I'm afraid he doesn't," said Billy's father. "He ought to thank God for the way he is made instead of saying that he just happened to grow by himself."

"He's like the gingerbread boy who ran away and thought he could do anything by himself," said Billy.

"That's right, Billy," said his father. "God gave that man his mind for thinking and his tongue for talking, but he used his tongue to say that there is no God."

"I thank God for having made me. He sure made me wonderful," said Billy.

"I'm glad you're thankful, Billy. So am I. It is God who has made us, and not we ourselves. That's what the Bible says, and it's true."

Let's talk about this: What did the big man say? What did Billy think of the man with the big voice? Why does our arm have a hand and not an ear? Why isn't our nose at the bottom of our foot? How else can we tell that God made us? Let's say the Bible verse together. Let's not forget that we belong to God. How can we show that we are thankful for our wonderful body?

Older children and grownups may now read: Psalm 100.

Let us thank God, our Maker, for the way He has made us: Dear Lord, we thank You for giving us eyes and ears, hands and feet, and a body that has the power to heal itself. We thank You especially for giving us a mind that can think. Forgive us for not always using our minds well, and keep us as Your children, for Jesus' sake. Amen.

Forgive one another. Ephesians 4:32b

How to Forgive Others

"I never want to see Dickie again," said Ruth. "He hurt me real bad."

"What did he do?" her mother asked.

"He told a lie about me. He said I never wash and never take a bath. And when we walked home, he hit a mud puddle with a stick and splashed mud all over my dress."

"But God wants us to forgive one another," said her mother. "Don't you want to forgive Dickie, too?"

Ruth looked down, stamped her foot, and said, "No! The next time I see him, I'll stick out my tongue at him. And the next time he asks me to help him in school, I'll tell him to go splash some mud on himself."

Ruth's mother looked at her for a while. Then she said, "If you can't forgive Dickie, I wonder why God told us to forgive one another."

Ruth hung her head, a little ashamed.

"God forgives us many things every day, Ruth dear," said her mother. "God forgives us our many sins for Jesus' sake. But He says He will not forgive us if we do not forgive others. Let's say the Lord's Prayer together. Perhaps Jesus will help us to forgive."

So the two prayed the Lord's Prayer. When they came to the part that says, "Forgive us our trespasses, as we forgive . . ." her mother stopped. "How do we want God to forgive us?" asked the mother.

"As we forgive," said Ruth. "As I forgive Dickie," she whispered.

After a while she said, "I'll forgive him, Mother, because Jesus wants me to." Then she felt better.

Let's think about this: Why didn't Ruth want to forgive Dickie? What did her mother ask her? When we pray the Lord's Prayer, how do we ask God to forgive us? Can you say the Bible verse? What made Ruth willing to forgive Dickie?

Bible reading for older children and grownups: Ephesians 4:30-32.

Let us bow and pray: Dear Father in heaven, You forgive all the sins we do, for Jesus' sake. Help us to forgive the few sins other people do against us, as You forgive us. Amen.

Trust in the Lord and do good. Psalm 37:3

God's Children Trust in Jesus

Linda was just learning to read. She read a Bible verse in her Sunday school lesson. It said, "Trust in the Lord and do good."

"Mother," she said, "what does 'trust' mean?"

Linda's mother lifted her to the kitchen table. Then she spread her arms and said, "Jump, Linda," the way she used to when Linda was smaller. Linda smiled and jumped.

207

"How did you know I wouldn't let you fall?" her mother asked.

"Oh, I knew," said Linda. "You'd never let me get hurt."

"See, you trust me, Linda. You jumped because you trusted me. If you had been afraid that I wouldn't catch you, you would not have jumped."

"Do I trust in the Lord when I think He will take care of me?" asked Linda.

"Yes, Darling," said her mother. "When you trust in God, you believe that He loves you and will take care of you."

"I trust God," said Linda.

"But don't forget the last part of the verse," said Linda's mother. "What else does it say God's children should do?"

Then Linda read the verse again. "I know," she said. "I should do what God wants me to do, because He will take care of me."

"Yes," said Linda's mother. "Trust in the Lord and do good. People who know how much the Lord Jesus loves them have a very good reason for doing what is right and good. People who do wrong to get something do not trust in the Lord."

Let's talk about trusting God: How did Linda's mother show her what "trust" means? What does "trust" mean? What can we be sure Jesus will do for us? How are we to show that we trust in the Lord?

Older children and grownups may now read: Psalm 37:1-5.

Let us pray together: Like a child trusts her mother, so will we trust You, dear Jesus, because You love us more than any mother ever loved her child. Please help us to show our trust in You by doing only what is good. Amen.

Jesus said, Where two or three are gathered together in My name, there am I in the midst of them. Matthew 18:20

The Meetings Jesus Attends

"Mother, I *have* to go to that meeting. Roy Rogers will be there," said Jim. He thought there was nobody as exciting as Roy Rogers.

So his mother said he could go.

The next Sunday morning Jim said, "Do I *have* to go to Sunday school and church?"

"Yes," said his mother. "Roy Rogers may be there."

"Will he really?" asked Jim.

"Would you go if he were?"

"Oh, sure," said Jim.

"Well," said his mother, "Roy Rogers probably won't be there, but there'll be Somebody more important."

"More important? Who?" asked Jim.

"The Lord Jesus will be there," his mother told him. "Jesus said, 'Where two or three are gathered together in My name, there am I in the midst of them.'"

"O. K.," said Jim. He didn't want to do less for Jesus than he would for Roy Rogers. Nobody is as important as Jesus, not even the most famous man in the world.

Does Jesus go to your church and Sunday school meetings? Oh, yes. The people who meet together at your church are Christians. They meet together as His disciples. Jesus said, "Where two or three are gathered together in My name, there am I in the midst of them." You won't want to miss seeing and hearing Him, will you?

Let's talk about this: Who did Jim think was the most important person in the world? Why did he want to go to a meeting? What great Person is at our Sunday school and

209

church every Sunday? Why will we want to go to Sunday school and church if we love Jesus? Who can say the Bible verse?

Older children and grownups may now read: John 20:18-20.

Let us pray to Jesus, who is with us now: Lord Jesus, help us to remember that whenever two or three or more of Your friends meet together, You are there with them. Then we will want to meet with them, too. Be with us in our home every day. Amen.

Has God forgotten to be gracious? Psalm 77:9

Will God Ever Forget Us?

First her little boy got sick and died. Then the father lost his job. Then somebody ran into their car and smashed it.

Mrs. Brown sat in her house and cried. "Has God stopped loving us?" she asked.

No, God never stops loving anyone. We don't always know why God lets some things happen to us. But God knows, and He never stops being gracious and good.

John Bunyan was put in jail for preaching about Jesus. In jail he wrote a book that helped many people believe in Jesus. So you see, God had a good reason for letting John Bunyan be put in jail.

The boy Joseph was sold as a slave in Egypt. There he became the ruler, and he saved many, many people from dying without food.

The man who wrote Psalm 77 was in great trouble. He prayed to God, but it seemed as though God didn't care about him. So he asked, "Has God forgotten to be gracious?

210

— Has He stopped loving us?" But then he remembered what God had done for him. So he said, "I will remember the works of the Lord."

Anyone who remembers how Jesus died for all people on a cross knows that God would never stop loving anybody. So if you ever wonder whether God has stopped loving you, think of what He did for you.

Let's talk about this: Why did Mrs. Brown sit and cry? Where did John Bunyan write a good book? How did God bless the boy Joseph in Egypt? If trouble will help us get to heaven, is it a good thing? Why can we be sure that God will never stop loving us?

Bible reading for older children and grownups: Psalm 77:7-15.

Let us pray together: Dear God, don't let us ever think that You are forgetting to love us. Help us to remember at all times how You saved us and made us Your children. We are glad that You keep on loving us for Jesus' sake. Amen.

The Lord is your Keeper. Psalm 121:5

God Watches over Us

Jane was a good baby sitter. She gave the best care to little children. One day Mrs. Gray said to Jane's mother, "I never worry when I have Janie stay with my children. I know I can trust her."

Jane saw to it that the children did not play too near the fireplace. She played with them to keep them from fighting with each other. She told them Bible stories and taught them to love Jesus. The children loved her because she loved them.

Did you know that we have somebody watching over us

211

all the time? The Bible says, "The Lord is your Keeper." God isn't a baby sitter, but in some ways Jane was like Him. He sees to it that we don't get hurt. He keeps us from doing wrong. He feeds us and gives us rest. He teaches us in the Bible and leads us to love Jesus, our Savior.

"The Lord is your Keeper," says the psalm verse. We are always safe when we are in God's care. We can trust Him more than the very best baby sitter. That's another reason why we love Him and want to be His children.

Let's talk about this: Why did Mrs. Gray like Jane? Why did the children love her? In what ways was Jane a little like God? What does our Bible verse say about the Lord? In what ways is God a better keeper than any baby sitter could be?

Older children and grownups may now recite or read: Psalm 121.

Let us thank God for watching over us: Dear God, we thank You for keeping watch over us and for loving us. We know that we often do wrong things. Please forgive our sins, and keep on loving us even though we do not deserve it. Please answer our prayer for Jesus' sake. Amen.

*Honor the Lord . . . with the first fruits . . . so shall
your barns be filled with plenty.* Proverbs 3:9, 10

Let's Think of God First

Mr. Smith got his check for a month's work. "But you
know," he told his friends, "after I paid the butcher and the
grocer and the man at the filling station and the bill for my
TV and a few more things, there wasn't much left for church!"

What was wrong with Mr. Smith? He did not remember
very well how much the Lord loved him. He put the Lord
in the wrong place. He put the Lord last. If Mr. Smith had
taken the Lord's share out of his check first, then he would
not have used up all the money on other things.

In the Old Testament part of the Bible, God told His
people to give the first fruits to Him. The first ripe grain
was to be the Lord's, and the first figs and the first calf and
the first lambs. Does God need figs and calves and lambs?
No, but God wants us to think of Him first, and He wants
us to love Him more than anything else. This is His first
Commandment.

A man once brought the prophet Elisha 20 small loaves
of bread for 100 students. It wasn't enough for so many, but
God blessed it and made it enough. Those 20 loaves were
his first fruits, the man said. He gave God His part first.

God promises to give us much more than we can ever
give to Him if we will think of Him first. So let's not forget
to honor the Lord by giving Him the first part of whatever
He gives us.

Let's talk about first fruits: Why didn't Mr. Smith have
money for his church? What should he have done? Which
fruits did God say He wants? Why does God want to be
first? What does He promise those who give Him their first

213

fruits? How can we give God the first part of the money we get?

Older children and grownups may now read: 2 Kings 4:42-44.

Let us pray: Dear Lord, we don't want to love our money or anything we have as much as we love You. Forgive us for being selfish with so much of what You give us. Help us to remember that we ought to give You the first part, because all of our blessings come from You. We ask this in the name of Jesus, our Savior. Amen.

Jesus said, I am the Light
of the world. John 9:5

Jesus Wants to Shine in Us

Everybody who came to church one evening got a candle. After the sermon the lights were turned off. The pastor lit his candle. "Will the ushers please light their candles from mine?" he said. They did that.

As the ushers went back down the aisle, they lighted the candles of the people sitting at the end of each bench. These people lighted the candles of the persons beside them; then the next person lighted his, and so on. Soon the whole church was bright with light. It all started from one candle.

Then the pastor told the people what it meant: The whole world is like a dark place. People are lost and can't see the right way to get to heaven. In the dark, people are also afraid and often do wrong things. But Jesus is like a bright light that is always burning. When we believe that He is our Savior, He begins to shine in us.

When Jesus shines in us, we become little lights, too. We

214

get light from Him. Then we can help light up the darkness around us. We can show people the way to heaven. We can tell them that Jesus is their Savior. We can also show them how to live right.

Are you a little light in the world? You will be if you love Jesus. He will shine in your heart, and others will see that you love Him and will come to love Him, too.

Let's talk about this: Where did all the little candles in the church get their light? In what ways do lights help people? Why do we say that people who do not know Jesus are lost in the dark? In what ways is Jesus like a light? How can we become lights? Let's say the Bible verse together; then try to say it alone.

Older children and grownups may now read: John 9:1-7.

Let us ask Jesus to shine in us: Dear Jesus, many people around us do not know You. They cannot see that You are their Savior, and they do not love You. Please shine in our hearts so that we will help to show others how wonderful You are. Amen.

With the Lord there is
    mercy. Psalm 130:7

Jesus Feels Sorry for Us

"Mercy sakes!" said little Jeanie. She had heard the neighbor lady say that. "Mommy, what does 'mercy' mean?" she asked.

" 'Mercy' means 'love,' Dear, like when somebody feels sorry that you hurt yourself, and tries to help you," her mother told her.

215

"Like when I fell out of a tree, and a man carried me home?" asked Jeanie.

"Yes," said her mother. "He showed mercy. But the most mercy is with the Lord Jesus."

"Why does Jesus feel sorry for us?" asked Jeanie.

"Because without His help we're in trouble," said her mother.

"What kind of trouble?" asked Jeanie.

"Well," said her mother, "we haven't always done what God wants us to do, have we?"

"No," answered Jeanie, "not always."

"Well," said her mother. "God is perfect and holy, and He can't allow His children to do wrong. He has to punish us for sinning."

"Oh," said Jeanie. "But Jesus saved us from being punished."

"How?" asked her mother, as if she didn't know.

"By having His Father punish Him instead of us," said Jeanie.

Jeanie was right. Jesus felt sorry for people because they were all in trouble with God. He died on a cross so that everyone could have forgiveness. "With the Lord there is mercy." That is why we love Him so very much.

Let's talk about this: What do you think the word "mercy" means? Why did the Lord Jesus feel sorry for all people? How did He help us all out of the trouble of sin? What is God willing to give us instead of punishment? Why is God willing to forgive us? Let's say the Bible verse together.

Bible reading for older children and grownups: Psalm 130.

Let us pray together: Dear Lord, heavenly Father, we know that we sin every day and deserve to be punished. But with You there is mercy, and we thank You for forgiving us our sins. Help us to be kind and good and true for Jesus' sake. Amen.

216

God says, Return to Me, for I have
redeemed you. Isaiah 44:22

We Belong to God

Jimmy's little dog ran away and went into a boy's yard down the street. The boy locked up the dog in his garage.

One day Jimmy was walking down the alley. He heard the little dog barking and begging to get out of the garage. Jimmy looked through the garage window and saw his dog.

But Jimmy knew that the boy would not give him back his dog. So he went to the boy and said, "I'll give you fifty cents for that dog." The bad boy wanted the fifty cents more than the dog, so he sold the dog back to Jimmy. We could say that Jimmy *redeemed* his dog. He bought him back. That's what "redeem" means — to buy back.

Do you know that we, too, were bought back? God made us, and we belong to Him. But like everybody else, we ran away from God by not loving Him and by doing wrong. We call that sinning. When people sin, the devil gets hold of them and tries to keep them as his children. Those who belong to the devil cannot get away from him by themselves.

But God bought us back. He redeemed us. Like the boy who bought his own dog back, God paid for us again. When

217

Jesus died for us on a cross, that was the price He paid to get us back as His children. Now anyone who wants to can have Jesus for his Savior and can be saved from sin and the devil. God says in the Bible, "Return to Me, for I have redeemed you."

Let's talk about this: What happened to Jimmy's dog when he ran away? How did Jimmy get his dog back? To whom do all people belong? When does the devil get hold of people? What did Jesus do to get us back to God? God wants all people to return to Him because He has paid to get them back. How can we return to God?

Bible reading for older children and grownups: Isaiah 44:21-23.

Let us pray: Thank You, God, for redeeming us and wanting us back even though we often run away from You and sin. Help us to remember how much You paid to have us as Your children, and keep us from getting caught by the devil. We ask this in Jesus' name. Amen.

Live in peace, and the God of love and peace will be with you. 2 Corinthians 13:11

Try to Get Along with Others

Have you ever set up dominoes or small blocks of wood one behind another? When the front block is pushed over, the whole row falls down. Why? Because each block hits the next one as it falls.

There is a way of stopping the whole row from falling. Just take one block out of the row, and that's where the hitting and falling will stop.

A quarrel is like a row of blocks. One person's words hit at the next person's words, and so they fall over each other.

218

Do you know how to stop a quarrel? Take out one angry bunch of words which hits at what the other person says. Say something friendly, or just don't say anything. See if that won't stop the quarrel.

Jesus said to His friends and followers, "Have peace with one another." That means, "Get along with one another." Our Bible verse says, "Live in peace." The opposite of peace is fighting, and quarrels are fighting with words.

Is it possible to live in peace with everybody? How about that mean boy who tries to start a fight? Or that hateful girl who is always stirring up trouble? Is a Christian supposed to let others be mean to him? No, not always. Sometimes we have to fight back in order to have peace. But the Bible says, "If it is possible, as much as you can, live in peace with everybody." God wants us to try as much as possible to get along with others.

God is Love, and God loves peace. When we love people and try to live in peace because we love Jesus, then the God of love and peace will be with us, says the Bible. He will be in our hearts.

Let's talk about this: What does it mean to "have peace" or to "live in peace" with one another? How can we often stop a quarrel? May we keep mean people from hurting us, or must we let others do what they please to us? What does God want us to try to do as much as possible? Who will help us to live in peace with other people? Why is God called the God of love and peace?

Bible reading for older children and grownups: Romans 12:14-21.

Let us pray together: Dear Father in heaven, please forgive all the quarreling and fighting we have done. Be with us in our hearts so that we will live in peace with other people as much as possible. We ask this because Jesus wants us to do so, and we want to be His children. Amen.

*Men ought always to pray and not
give up.* Luke 18:1

Why Keep On Praying?

Once there was a judge who didn't care about people at all. He didn't even care about God. One day a widow came to him. "Please help me," she begged. "My enemy is trying to harm me."

The judge said, "Don't bother me. I don't have time for you." So the poor old woman went away.

But the next day she came back to the judge and asked again. Once more he told her to go home. But she came back the next day and the next day and the next day. She kept coming day after day. She didn't leave him alone. She didn't give up asking.

At last the wicked judge said, "I don't care about God, and I don't care about this widow, but because she keeps on bothering me, I will help her; otherwise she will wear me out." So the wicked judge helped her in order to get rid of her.

After Jesus had told this story, He said, "Remember what this wicked judge said and did. Will not God give help to His own people who keep on praying to Him day and night? I tell you, He will hurry to help them."

So Jesus wants us to keep on praying, even when God doesn't seem to help us right away. He loves us and will surely answer our prayers more quickly than a wicked judge would.

Let's talk about this: What did a widow ask a judge? Why didn't the judge want to help her at first? Why did he help her? Why did Jesus tell the story about the widow and the judge? Why is God always willing to help us? Why doesn't He always help us right away?

220

Bible reading for older children and grownups: Luke 18:1-8.

Let us pray: Dear Lord, please help us in all our troubles. Teach us to pray to You for help and to keep on praying to You when we need help. We know that You love us, and we are glad that You have promised to answer our prayers. Please hear our prayers for Jesus' sake. Amen.

Jesus went about doing good. Acts 10:38

Imitating Jesus

Boy Scouts are told to do one good deed every day. Do you think that Jesus was satisfied with doing only one good deed a day? The Bible says, "Jesus went about doing good." Wherever He went, He did good; and whatever He did was good.

What are some of the things we could do in order to be like Jesus? Let's think of some of the things He did:

Jesus worked. He was a carpenter. He made things that

221

other people could use. Jesus wants us to work. Even children can help their parents with work that needs to be done. They can also do good work at school. Let's remember that we can do good by working.

Jesus helped the sick. We can't heal the sick, but we can pray for them, cheer them up, and sometimes do other things for them. Some children might become doctors or nurses. Like Jesus, our Lord, we can do good by helping the sick.

When people were hungry, Jesus gave them something to eat. Jesus wants us to feed the hungry. He said that when we give food to hungry people because we love Him, we are doing good to Him. Remember, we can do good by feeding those who are hungry.

Jesus helped people learn about God. Whenever He had a chance, He talked to people about His Father in heaven and about Himself and how people could become God's children. We can do good by talking to other children and grownups about Jesus, by taking people to Sunday school and church, and by helping people learn God's Word in other ways.

Jesus went about doing good. To be like Jesus, we will want to do as much good as we can every day.

Let's talk about this: What does our Bible verse say Jesus did wherever He went? What were some of the good things Jesus did? In which ways can we help the sick? How can we help people to learn more about God and the way to heaven? Why do Christians want to do as much good as possible?

Bible reading for older children and grownups: Acts 10:36-43.

Let us pray together: Dear heavenly Father, we want to be like Jesus. Please forgive us for not ever doing as much good as we could. Help us to grow up doing good as Jesus did. In His name we ask this. Amen.

Let us not grow weary
in welldoing. Galatians 6:9

Don't Quit Doing Good

A man on the radio was helping people get jobs. Out of the first thousand people for whom he got jobs, how many do you think said "Thank you"? Only ten. Should he quit trying to help people just because they weren't thankful?

Jesus once came to a place where there were ten very sick lepers. Doctors were not able to heal lepers in those days. There was no hope for these men. They begged Jesus to help them, and Jesus did. He made them well. How many came back to give thanks to Jesus? Only one. Did Jesus quit doing good because people were not thankful?

Jesus never gets tired of being good to people. To whom does He do good now yet? To you and to me and to all of us. We often forget to thank Him. We even disobey Him in many ways every day. You'd think He would get tired of doing good to us. But He keeps right on forgiving us and loving us and helping us.

So why should we get tired of helping other people? "Let us not grow weary (or tired) in welldoing," says the Bible. If people do not appreciate what we do for them, remember, most people didn't thank Jesus either, and they still don't. Even we don't. But Jesus keeps right on being good to us all, and He wants us never to get tired of doing good.

Let's talk about doing good: How many people said thanks to the radio man? How many lepers came back to thank Jesus? Who never gets tired of doing good? To whom does He do good? What does the Bible verse tell us?

Older children and grownups may now read: Galatians 6:1-10.

Let us pray together: Dear Jesus, we are glad that You never get tired of doing good to us. Please help us to show our thanks by never getting tired of doing good to other people. Amen.

Let all bitterness and wrath and anger and clamor
and evil speaking be put away from you. Ephesians 4:31

Something Christians Get Rid Of

When little George didn't get what he wanted right away, he'd scream. If his mother didn't come running, he screamed real hard. He found that if he screamed hard enough and got red in the face, his mother would do anything he wanted.

So George learned to get his way by becoming angry and making a lot of noise. He would lose his temper whenever his playmates didn't play his way. He would say mean things even about his friends when they didn't do what he wanted.

George grew up and got married. Always he had to have his way. When his wife and children didn't obey him at once, he would throw things at them and yell at them and hit them. His wife became afraid of him, and his children did not love him.

What if God, our Father in heaven, were like that? What if He became angry and punished us every time we didn't do what He wants? He'd be punishing us all the time, wouldn't He?

But the Bible says, "The Lord is slow to anger." Because God is good and full of love, He is kind and forgiving. He sent His Son Jesus to die for us on a cross so that He wouldn't have to punish us.

And God wants His children to be like Him. That's why He says, "Let all bitterness and wrath [bad temper] and

224

anger [hatred] and clamor [noise] and evil speaking [mean talk] be put away from you."

Let's talk about this: What did George do to get his way when he was little? Why were his wife and children afraid of him? What if God would become angry at us for not doing what He wants? Why is God slow to anger and willing to forgive us? That is why we love Him. What does He say we should put away in order to be like Him?

Bible reading for older children and grownups: Psalm 145:1-8.

Let us pray together: Dear Lord God, it is wonderful to know that You are full of love and slow to anger, because we sin much and deserve to be punished by You every day. Please continue to love us for the sake of Jesus, our Savior, and help us to get rid of all anger and loud and mean talk. In Jesus' name we ask this. Amen.

Thou shalt not steal. Exodus 20:15

God's Law Is Good

"Why is it wrong to steal?" Bobby asked his mother. "I wish it were all right to steal. Then I could take candy from the store when I want to."

That night Bobby had a dream. He dreamed that it wasn't wrong to steal. In his dream he went to a store and took some candy. He also took some apples and some potato chips.

The next day he went to the store again. It was empty. People had stolen everything. The store man had locked the store and put up a sign. It said, "For sale." Nobody would be a store man if stealing were right.

Bobby came home and asked his mother for an ice-cream

225

cone. "We can't get any ice cream," said his mother. "All the ice cream has been stolen. The ice-cream man can't sell ice cream any more. Everybody takes it when he has some."

Then Bobby went out to ride his tricycle. It was gone. He ran back into the house. "Mother," he said, "somebody stole my tricycle."

His mother said, "It's all right to steal what belongs to somebody else."

Bobby started to cry. He didn't like what stealing did to him. He wished everybody would obey God's Commandment. Then he woke up. It was only a dream. He looked out of the window. There was his tricycle in the yard. "Mommy," he said, "I don't ever want to steal anything."

"I'm glad," said his mother. "God knows what is best for us. That's why He told us not to steal."

Let's talk about this: Which law did Bobby want to change? What happened in his dream? Who gave us the law "Thou shalt not steal"? Why is it a good law? What does the Bible call the breaking of God's laws? How can we get forgiveness of our sins?

Bible reading for older children and grownups: Romans 2:21-24.

Let us pray: Thank You for giving us Your laws, dear God. Help us to keep them, and when we break any, please forgive us for Jesus' sake. Amen.

*Jesus said, You are the salt
of the earth.* Matthew 5:13

What Good Salt Does

"Jim is a pickle-puss," said Larry.

"And Larry is a salt barrel," said Jim. They were just teasing; they weren't quarreling.

"I know I'm salt," said Larry. "And so are you. Jesus said so."

"He did?" asked Jim, a little surprised. "What did He say?"

"Jesus said, 'You are the salt of the earth,'" Larry told Jim. "Jesus meant us, too, didn't He, Dad?" asked Larry as his father walked into the room.

"Yes," said his father. "He meant all of His disciples, and that includes also the people who believe in Him and love Him today. But do you know how we are to be salt?"

The boys didn't know, so Larry's father sat down and explained it to them. "You know," he said, "when I was a boy on a farm, my mother had a pork barrel. We didn't have a refrigerator, so she would put our meat into the barrel. Then she would put a lot of salt on it. The salt kept the meat from getting rotten. It kept the worms out.

"Jesus wants us to keep the people around us from getting rotten. He wants us to help people to become God's children so that they will live good lives. When we tell others about Jesus and when we give them a good example by the way we behave, then we are like good salt. Let's not forget, Jesus wants us to be good salt."

Thinking about this: For what was salt used in a meat barrel long ago? Why did Jesus call His people salt? How can we help to save people around us? How does faith in

Jesus keep people from becoming rotten? Let's say the Bible verse together.

Older children and grownups may now read and memorize: Matthew 5:13-16.

Let us pray: Dear Jesus, we want to be salt. Help us to bring many people into Your kingdom and make each one of us a good Christian example for all those around us. Amen.

I will live in the house of the Lord forever. Psalm 23:6

Going to God's House

Mrs. Brown was crying because her little girl Betty had died. For the funeral they put Betty into a pretty box. Later they took her to the cemetery. There they put her down into a grave. She would never come back to play or to hug her mother and say, "I love you." She was dead. So Mrs. Brown cried.

Mr. Brown said, "Don't cry, Ann. Betty is in heaven. Only her body is dead. Betty is in the house of the Lord. It's a beautiful place. And Jesus is there with her, taking good care of her."

"Yes, I know," said Mrs. Brown and tried to smile. "But I'm lonesome for her."

"We'll see her again in the house of the Lord," said Mr. Brown.

As Mr. and Mrs. Brown grew older, they often said, "Dear Jesus, please take us to Your home in heaven someday. We want to be with You and Betty always." And they knew Jesus would take them, because the Lord Jesus was their Savior and Shepherd.

They often said the Twenty-third Psalm together. They liked the last words best of all: "I will live in the house of the Lord." Whenever they said these words, they thought of the little girl Betty and the time when they would be with her and Jesus in heaven.

Let's talk about this: What happened to Betty Brown? Where did Jesus take Betty after she died? When did her parents expect to see Betty again? Who takes people to heaven when they die? Why is heaven called "the house of the Lord"? Can you say the Bible verse Betty's parents liked to say?

Older children and grownups may now read: Psalm 23.

Let us pray together: Thank You, Lord Jesus, for all that You have done so that we can someday be in heaven with You. We thank You for dying on the cross to save us. We want You to be our Savior so that we, too, will live with You forever in heaven. Amen.

In the day of my trouble I will call on God, for He will answer me. Psalm 86:7

Jesus Always Helps

"I'm afraid to tell Mr. Gruff that I broke his garage window," said Allan. The boys had been throwing stones at tin cans on Mr. Gruff's fence posts. One of Allan's stones had gone too far.

"You're in real trouble, aren't you?" said his sister. "Did he see you?"

"No," said Allan, "but I keep thinking about it. Jesus knows I did it. But if I tell Mr. Gruff, he may get angry."

"Why don't you ask Jesus what to do?" his sister asked.

"Oh," said Allan. "I already know what He wants me to do. He wants me to tell the truth and to pay for what I broke. But how can I?"

"Why don't you ask Jesus to help you?" said his sister.

So Allan thought some more and also prayed to Jesus. "Dear Jesus, help me to do what's right," he prayed. Then he went over to Mr. Gruff's house and knocked on the door.

Mrs. Gruff answered. "We were throwing rocks and one of mine broke your garage window," said Allan. "I'm very sorry, and I'll pay for it," he said, shaking a little.

"Well," said Mrs. Gruff, "it's very nice that you were willing to tell me. The carpenter is coming today to make some storm windows. I'll have him put in that window first, and you may pay me when you can."

Allan felt very much better when he heard that. He thanked Mrs. Gruff, and on the way home he thanked Jesus. He knew that Jesus had helped him do what was right and that Jesus had made it turn out all right.

Let's talk about this: What was Allan's trouble? What did his sister tell him to do? What was the right thing for Allan to do? Why? How did Jesus help Allan do what was right? How did it turn out?

Older children and grownups may now read: Psalm 86:3-12.

Let us pray: Thank You, dear Jesus, for always helping us when we call on You in trouble. We thank You especially for helping us to get out of the trouble of sin by forgiving us. We love You for that more than anything. Amen.

Now are we the children of God. 1 John 3:2

God's Children

Like Cinderella, a poor little orphan girl once had to work hard for the people with whom she stayed. She had to do the things nobody else wanted to do, and she got very little pay for it.

One day a king and his son visited the farm where the little girl worked, and the king's son fell in love with her. "Don't tell anybody," he whispered to her. "Someday I will come back for you and marry you."

The girl kept right on doing her work, but now she was happy and cheerful and sang all day long. Nobody knew why she was so happy, but she knew: she was going to be married to a prince and would be a child of the king.

We are all like that girl. For a while we live here on earth. We may have hard work and many troubles. But Jesus, God's Son, came to visit us on earth, and He promised to come back and take us to His Father's home in heaven. God adopted us as His children because His Son Jesus loves

231

us and wants us to be with Him in heaven. That's the reason we can be happy and cheerful at all times.

"Now are we the children of God," says the Bible, and that's wonderful to know. But the Bible says it will be even more wonderful when we will be with Jesus in heaven.

Let's talk about this: Why was the little girl happy even though she had to work hard? Whose Son came from heaven and promised to take us there? Because Jesus loves us and we love Jesus, what does the heavenly Father call us? How will we act if we really believe that we are God's children?

Older children and grownups may now read: 1 John 3:1-5.

Let us pray together: Dear God, we are glad that You call us Your children for Jesus' sake. We are glad that You forgive all our sins because Jesus died for us. We know that Jesus is coming to take us to heaven. Help us to remember this so that we will be ready and waiting. We ask this in Jesus' name. Amen.

O Lord, how great are Your works! Psalm 92:5

God Is Great and Good

In California there was a man who studied the stars. He looked through a big telescope and saw that there were millions of stars, some much bigger than the earth. Some of these stars moved around, but they never bumped into one another. Every star had its own place or path. The man could tell where any star would be a year later. The man said, "Surely this is the work of God. Who else could have planned all this?"

232

Then there was a man who studied germs. He would put a drop of water under a microscope. The microscope made the drop of water look almost as big as a dinner plate. Through the microscope the man could see all kinds of tiny bugs swimming around in the drop of water. "Look at those germs," he said; "millions of them in a drop of water. And they all live until it is time for them to die. O Lord, how great are Your works!"

A young woman rode on a train through the Rocky Mountains. As she looked out of the window, she said, "O Lord, how great are Your works!" A boy once caught some snow on his gloves. He noticed that every flake of snow was different. He remembered the words, "O Lord, how great are Your works!"

These are just a few of the people who understood and believed what the psalm writer said long ago in the Bible. And the greatest thing God ever did was to send His Son Jesus to be our Savior. O Lord, how great are Your works!

Let's talk about God's works: What did one man see through a telescope? What did another see in a drop of water? What great work of God did a young woman see from a train window? What made the boy think of God? What is the greatest work God has done for us? What is so wonderful about that?

Older children and grownups may now read: Psalm 92:1-5.

Let us praise God together in prayer: All that You have ever done, Lord God, honors You, and we praise You for all Your wonderful works. Especially do we thank and praise You for sending Jesus to die for our sins. Make and keep us as Your dear children every day for Jesus' sake. Amen.

How sweet are God's words to my taste; yes, sweeter than honey to my mouth! Psalm 119:103

God's Word Is Sweet

A man was standing on a high bridge. He was having much trouble. His little boy had fallen out of his car and had been killed. His wife blamed him and wouldn't live with him any more. He didn't think anybody loved him, so he decided to jump off the bridge and drown himself. That's how bad he felt.

As he stood looking down at the water, the wind blew a little piece of paper to his feet. On the paper were three words, "God loves you."

The man sat down and cried. He cried because he was happy. He was thinking of some of the Bible words he had learned once in a Christian school. "God so loved the world that He gave His only-begotten Son." "He loved me and gave Himself for me." These were some of God's words he remembered.

That man tasted how sweet the Word of God is, more than most of us ever do. When a man in a desert doesn't have water for two days and then finds water, how good the water tastes to him! When a person thinks that nobody loves him and then remembers how Jesus died for him on a cross, that's when God's words seem extra sweet, sweeter than honey.

But all of God's children love to hear and learn God's Word, because they want to hear and learn more about Jesus, their sweet Savior. God's words are sweet, and to those who love Jesus they seem sweeter than honey.

Let's talk about this: What was the man on the bridge going to do? Why? What did the wind bring to him? Why did he cry? When does God's Word seem extra sweet to people? Why do all of God's children love His Word? Which is your favorite Bible verse?

Bible reading for older children and grownups: Psalm 119:97-104.

Let us pray: Thank You, dear Father in heaven, for the sweet message that You love us and want us to be Your children. Your promises of forgiveness and life in heaven are sweeter than honey. Teach us to love Your words so that we will learn more and more of them and may never forget them. We ask this in Jesus' name. Amen.

With everlasting kindness will I have mercy on you, says the Lord. Isaiah 54:8

God's Kindness Never Stops

Buddy loved to go over to see the new neighbor lady, because she talked to him and gave him cookies and soda pop.

One day Buddy stepped off the porch and right on top of the lady's best flowers. "I didn't mean to," he told her.

But she became very angry. "Get off my place," she told Buddy, "and don't ever come back."

Buddy ran home. He was scared. He ran and told his father what the lady had said.

"I'm glad you didn't do it on purpose," said his father. "I'll go and talk to her. Maybe we can get her some new flowers."

"She was so nice on other days," said Buddy. "Why would she be so mean all of a sudden?"

"Oh, she just lost her temper," said his father. "Aren't you glad that God isn't like that? The Bible says His kindness lasts forever."

"Jesus would have said, 'I know you didn't mean to do it, Buddy,' and He would have forgiven me," said Buddy.

"Yes," said his father, "I'm sure He would have. He forgives us many things every day, and His kindness never ends."

Let's talk about this: What did the new neighbor lady say to Buddy one day? Why? What did Buddy's father say he would do? Who never stops being kind and forgiving? What did Buddy think Jesus would say to anyone who is sorry for what he does wrong? Why?

Bible reading for older children and grownups: Isaiah 54:7-13.

Let us pray together: Thank You, dear Lord, our loving God, for always being kind to us and ready to forgive. Please help us always to be kind and good to others for Jesus' sake. Amen.

The will of the Lord be done. Acts 21:14

Letting God Decide Things

It was no fun to be in jail in the days when the Apostle Paul was preaching about Jesus. Jails were like dirty cellar rooms, and prisoners were treated very roughly.

One time Paul was on his way to Jerusalem. On the way he stopped to visit a friend. There the prophet Agabus came to see him. He took Paul's belt and tied his own hands and feet with it. Then he said, "The Holy Spirit has told me that the people in Jerusalem will tie up the man who owns this belt, and will give him to the soldiers."

Then the friends of Paul said to him, "Don't go to Jerusalem. Please don't go." But Paul said, "What are you trying to do by crying and breaking my heart? I want God's will to be done, even if I have to go to jail. I am willing even to die for Jesus."

When the friends of Paul saw that he would not change his mind, they quit begging him not to go. They said, "The will of the Lord be done."

Sometimes we wish that things could be different from what they are. If we love God, we will try to change what we can make better. But some things cannot be changed, and sometimes we do not know what is best. God always knows what is best, so we can always say, "The will of the Lord be done." Whatever He wants is best, because He loves us. He will not let anything really hurt us.

Let's talk about this: What did the prophet Agabus say would happen to Paul? What did the friends of Paul beg him not to do? What did Paul say he was willing to do for Jesus' sake? When the friends of Paul saw that they could

237

not keep him from going to Jerusalem, what did they say? Why are Christians willing to let God decide things?

Older children and grownups may now read: Acts 21:10-15.

Let us pray together: Dear Lord God, help us to say, "The will of the Lord be done," no matter what may happen to us. As long as You decide things for us, we know that everything will turn out all right. Amen.

He who has pity on the poor lends to the Lord; and that which he has given will He pay him again. Proverbs 19:17

What God Wants to Borrow

There was a beggar in New York who got rich by begging. When he died, they found stockings and coats and drawers stuffed with money in his room. Some beggars are liars, and we don't have to help them. We should be careful to help those who really need it. When we give to those who do not need it, we are wasting our gifts.

But there are many people in the world who are very poor. They need help. Many of them have run away from Communists and have nothing. We can help some of them come to this country, and we can help them where they are.

There are people in India who hardly ever have a full meal. Many children are very thin because they do not get enough to eat. Some die from being hungry.

Also in our country there are people who are poor because they are old or sick and cannot work.

When we give to the poor because we love Jesus, it is the same as if we were lending it to the Lord. Do you know
238

why? The Lord promises that He will pay us back when we help the poor. He who is kind to the poor lends to the Lord. That's what the Bible verse tells us. So let's be kind to the poor.

Let's talk about this: Do you know of any poor people who may need our help? What can we do for them? Can you say at least the first part of the Bible verse? To whom do we lend what we give to the poor? What does the Bible promise to those who give to the poor?

Bible reading for older children and grownups: Deuteronomy 24:19-21.

Let us pray: Thank You for all the good things we have received from You, dear Father in heaven. Please give us tender hearts so that we will gladly help those who need our help. We ask this in Jesus' name, because He gave us His life and wants us to pity the poor. Amen.

I have no greater joy than to hear that my children walk in truth. 3 John 4

Happy People

"How are you, my boy?" said Mr. Jones. "Fine," said Freddy. Then he went into the house. "Mother," he asked, "why does Mr. Jones call me his boy? I'm not his boy."

"Oh, many grown-up people talk that way," said his mother. "It means that he likes you, as if you were his boy."

In our Bible verse the disciple John was writing to people who were not his children, but he called them his children. He loved them as though they were his children. And in one way they were his children. He had taught them God's Word. He had been their pastor and teacher.

One day he got a letter saying, "Your Christians in Ephesus are kind to poor people." That made him very happy. Then somebody told him, "Your church members are good to the people who are working for Jesus." That made him happy. He knew then that they loved Jesus. That's why he wrote, "I have no greater joy than to hear that my children walk in truth."

To walk in truth means to do what God has said. It means believing and doing what the Bible teaches. Our ministers and teachers and our parents are glad, too, when they see their "children" walk in the truth. Nothing makes them happier than to see their children growing up to be good Christians.

But we will walk in the truth only if we will keep on learning the truth. That's why it's so important for all of us to study the Bible in our home, to go to Sunday school and Bible class regularly, to attend a Christian day school and high school if we can, and go to church together every time we can.

Let's talk about this: What are some of the things people believe when they walk in the truth? What are some of the things they do? In what book can we find the truth about Jesus and His teachings? What will help us to keep on being Christians? How do the people who love Jesus feel when they see that we love Him?

Bible reading for older children and adults: 3 John 2-4 and 11.

Let us pray together: Dear Jesus, help us to follow You, for we know that You are the only true Way to heaven. Keep us as Your children so that our parents and all who love You will always be happy over us. Amen.

240

By love serve one another. Galatians 5:13

Serving Others as Jesus Did

"Mother, please get me a drink of water," said Ruth when she was sick in bed. Her mother was glad to do it. She served Ruth by getting her a glass of water.

When Ruth was well again, she became a wee bit lazy. "Mother, please get me a drink of water," she said. This time she could have gotten it herself, but she did not want to walk over to the kitchen faucet.

"No, Honey, I don't think I had better," said her mother. "You may learn to let other people serve you, and that's the wrong way to a happy and good life. The Bible says we should serve one another. That means we should be ready to help others, not always wait to be helped."

So Ruth got herself a drink of water. Then she said, "Mother, shall I bring you one, too?"

"Yes, please," said her mother. Her mother was glad that Ruth was willing to serve.

If a mother always does everything for her children, how will they learn to work or to help others? Ruth's mother served Ruth when Ruth was sick. She was glad to serve. But she also helped Ruth learn to serve.

241

God wants us to be helpful to other people, to love them enough to serve them. Jesus said, "That's the way to become great in My kingdom — by serving others." He said, "Be like Me. I gave My life for people."

Let's see what we have learned: How did Ruth's mother serve her when she was sick? Why didn't her mother do it when Ruth was well? What does "serve" mean? What does our Bible verse tells us? How did Jesus serve people when He was on earth? What did He say was the only way to become great?

Bible reading for older children and grownups: Matthew 20:25-28.

Let us pray: Dear Jesus, we know that You died on a cross in order to serve us. We ought to be ashamed not to love other people enough to help them. Please forgive us for wanting to be served instead of serving. Help us to become great by serving others for Your sake. Amen.

Jesus came to save the lost. Luke 19:10

Helping Jesus to Save the Lost

Tom had gone just a short way into a woods. Now he couldn't find his way back. He cried and called, but nobody answered. He was lost.

Then Tom said to himself, "I had better stay here. Somebody will come looking for me. My dad will."

So he went to the top of a hill and sat down. Soon he heard his father calling him. Was Tom ever glad to be found when he was lost!

Many people are far away from God and are lost. They think they are going to heaven, but they are going the wrong way. Jesus is looking for them. He came to find the lost people in order to save them.

Jesus has found us and saved us. Without Him we would all be lost. Every time we sin we walk away from God. But Jesus calls us back. He even died for us on a cross in order to save us. And God forgives us on account of what Jesus did for us.

Many people do not know about Jesus, and some do not care. They are still lost. Jesus wants to find them. He wants to save them, too.

But how does Jesus do it? Through the people who have been found. He does it when *we* tell others that Jesus is their Savior. Those who believe us and follow Jesus are saved. They are brought back to God. When they die, they go to heaven. So we can help to save the lost. That is what Jesus wants us to do for Him.

Let's talk about this: In what way was Tommy lost? How do people become lost on the way to heaven? What did Jesus do to save all people? How do we know whether Jesus has found us? How can we help to save others who are lost?

Bible reading for older children and grownups: Luke 19:1-10.

Let us pray: Dear Jesus, we are glad that You found us and are taking us to heaven. We want to help find others who are lost so that they, too, will be saved. Please help us. Amen.

Jesus said, Be happy; it is I;
don't be afraid. Matthew 14:27

Don't Be Afraid

Peggy screamed. It was nighttime, and she was having a bad dream. In her dream a big, ugly animal came out of the clouds. She thought it was going to eat her. Her mother woke her up and said, "Don't be afraid, Peggy. I'm here, and you're all right."

But Peggy was afraid to go back to sleep. So her mother told her the story about Jesus walking on the water. The friends of Jesus were in a boat. There was a big storm. They were having trouble. It was dark. All at once they saw something walking on the water.

Some of the men screamed. They were afraid. They thought it was a spook or a ghost. They thought it might hurt them.

Then they heard a voice. It said, "Be happy; it is I; don't be afraid." At first they wouldn't believe it was Jesus. But when Jesus came into their boat, they were happy.

After Peggy's mother told her the story, she said, "Peggy, in a dream we sometimes see scary things, just as the friends of Jesus did in the dark. But when they knew that Jesus was with them, they weren't afraid any more. Jesus is by our bed also in the dark. He is with us, no matter where we are. And when we are afraid, He also says to us, 'Be happy . . . don't be afraid.'"

"I'm not afraid any more," said Peggy. Then she put her pretty head back on the pillow and soon was asleep again.

Let's talk about this: What scared Peggy? What scared the friends of Jesus? What sometimes scares people today? Where is Jesus whenever we are afraid? What did Jesus say when His friends were afraid? Why can Jesus always help us? How can we help anybody who is afraid?

Bible reading for older children and grownups: Matthew 14:22-33.

Let us pray: Dear Jesus, please help us to get over being afraid. Help us to remember that You are always with us and will keep us from anything that would really hurt us. Help us always to be cheerful, because we know that You love us. Amen.

How often shall my brother sin against me and I forgive him? Till seven times? Matthew 18:21

Seventy Times Seven

"I'm never going to speak to him again," said Martha. She was angry because her brother Jerry had called her a cat.

"Aren't God's children supposed to forgive one another?" asked Martha's mother.

"I'm tired of forgiving him," said Martha. "Why do I always have to forgive?"

"Martha," said her mother, "the disciple Peter once came to Jesus and said, 'Lord, how often do I have to forgive somebody who sins against me? Is seven times often enough?' What do you think Jesus answered? Jesus said, 'Not seven times, but seventy times seven.'"

Why do you think Jesus said seventy times seven? Because hardly ever would anybody sin against us that often. Jesus meant that we should always be willing to forgive, no matter how often somebody does something wrong against us.

Then Jesus told Peter a story. He said, "Once there was

245

a man who owed his king more than he could ever pay back. So the king decided to sell the man and his wife and children. Kings could do such things in those days. But when the man begged the king not to do it, the king forgave him and said he would not have to pay anything at all.

"The man was glad. But then the man went and put another man into prison just because the other man owed him a little and couldn't pay right away. When the king heard about this, he was angry. He told his soldiers to bring the unkind man back to him. The king said to him, 'You wicked servant, I forgave you all that you owed me. Couldn't you have been good to others as I was good to you?' So the king put the wicked man into jail and said, 'Stay there until you have paid everything to me!'"

Then Jesus said, "That's the way My heavenly Father will treat you if you are not willing to forgive other people their sins." Our Father in heaven is willing to forgive all our sins all the time. But He expects us to do the same for other people.

Let's talk about this: What did Peter think would be enough times to forgive? How often does Jesus expect us to forgive a person? What did Jesus mean when He said, "Seventy times seven"? How much did the king forgive the wicked servant? How much has God forgiven us? Why was the servant punished? What will we be willing to do if we appreciate God's forgiveness?

Bible reading for older children and grownups: Matthew 18:23-35.

Let us pray: Dear heavenly Father, we are thankful that You have forgiven us thousands of times and that You are willing to forgive us for Jesus' sake. Please give us the Holy Spirit so that we will always be willing to forgive other people for Jesus' sake. Amen.

*Jesus said, He who has seen Me has seen
the Father.* John 14:9

Seeing What God Is Like

Two children were out in their back yard one summer night. Each one had a flashlight and was shining it into the dark places. All at once the boy pointed his toward the sky. "I wish I could see God," he said.

The girl held her flashlight up, too. She said, "So do I."

One time when Jesus was on earth, His friend Philip wished that, too. He said to Jesus, "Lord, show us the Father, and we will all be glad."

Jesus said to him, "He who has seen Me has seen the Father." Jesus, the Son of God, is exactly like His Father, so those who know Jesus know what God is like.

What was Jesus like when He was on earth? The Bible tells us. He was kind and good. He loved children. He could do anything. He helped people. He taught people to be sorry for what they do wrong, and He wanted them to live in His kingdom. He even died on a cross to pay for all sins so that we could be with Him in heaven.

Have you ever wished you could see God? We cannot see Him with the eyes of our body, but we can see Him with the eyes of our mind. Jesus said, "He who has seen Me has seen the Father." We can see what Jesus is like by reading the Bible or by hearing and learning Bible stories about Jesus.

Let's talk about this: Whom did the children with the flashlights wish they could see? What did Jesus tell His friend Philip when he asked to see God? How can we get to know Jesus? What was Jesus like when He was on earth? Who can say the Bible verse from memory?

Older children and grownups may read: John 14:6-12.

Let us pray together: Dear God, we know how good and kind Jesus is and how much He loves us. We are glad that You are just like Him. Help us to learn more about Him so that we will know You better and love You more. We ask this as His dear children. Amen.

As newborn babes, desire the sincere milk of the Word, that you may grow thereby. 1 Peter 2:2

What Makes Christians Grow?

"How tall am I now, Mother?" Donny asked almost every day. Donny wished he could grow faster. Sometimes his mother would put him against a wall and measure him. Then Donny would stand on his tiptoes in order to be as big as possible. Donny wanted to grow fast.

"Eat your vegetables and drink your milk, and God will make you a grown-up man soon," said his mother.

Vegetables and milk are good for growing tall, but tall is not the only way to grow. God wants us to grow also in knowing the Lord. He wants us to become grown-up Christians. The Bible says, "Grow in grace and in the knowledge of our Lord and Savior Jesus Christ."

How can we grow in knowing the Lord? By learning Bible verses and by doing what they say. By going to Sunday school and to other schools which our church has for us. By listening to the minister in the church services. By having family devotions every day. By reading Bible story books, and by reading the Bible when we are old enough to do so. By doing what we learn from the Bible. And by talking about God with our parents, teachers, and friends.

So you see, we grow in the knowledge of our Lord and Savior Jesus Christ by learning God's Word, the Bible. Our Bible verse says that God's Word is like milk. This milk helps us to grow as Christians. That is why we should want it just like a new baby wants milk for his body. Milk makes us grow, doesn't it? And so does the Word of God.

Let's talk about this: What helps our body grow? How can we grow in knowing the Lord Jesus? Knowing about Jesus and His teachings is important. What is even more important? How can we grow up to be bigger and better Christians?

Bible reading for older children and grownups: Acts 18:24-26.

Let us pray together: Dear Lord Jesus, we want to grow into bigger and better Christians. Please bless our Bible lessons so that we will learn to know You better. And give us the Holy Spirit so that we will love You and become more and more like You. Amen.

Whatever things are lovely; whatever things are of good report . . . think about these things. Philippians 4:8

What to Think About

There is a story about a man who was very mean and ugly. He did not like things that were pretty, and he lived all alone in a dark old house.

Then one day the man fell in love with a young girl. She was sweet and friendly and very beautiful. He wanted to marry her, but she said, "I will never marry a man whose face is not lovely."

So the man bought a mask which made him look like a kind and good person. He also did his best to be good to the girl, and together they did lovely things. They read good books together, they listened to beautiful music, they walked together in the parks and enjoyed God's pretty birds and flowers.

After a while they were married, and they were very happy. But one day an old enemy came to the man's house. He tore the mask off the man's face in front of his wife. The man tried to hide his face, because he didn't want his wife to see how ugly he was. But when he looked into a mirror, he saw that his face had become like that of the person he had tried to be.

This isn't a true story, but it has a true meaning. The Bible tells us to think of whatever is lovely and good. If we will do that, we will become more and more like Jesus. Even our face will become more sweet and beautiful if He is in our mind and heart.

Let's talk about this: What changed the ugly man's face? What does God want His children to think about? How can we tell what is in some people's minds and hearts? Why

250

will we not look mean if Jesus is in our heart? How will we look? Why does God want us to think of the things that are good?

Bible reading for older children and adults: Philippians 4:4-9.

Let us pray together: Dear Father in heaven, we know that You are good and that everything You think and do is good. We thank You for loving us and sending Jesus to save us from our sins. Please help us to be lovely and good, and make us what You want us to be, through Jesus, our Savior. Amen.

Love . . . is kind. 1 Corinthians 13:4

What Love Does

"Mother," said Janie, "Louise has a haircut, and does it ever look funny."

"Funny?" asked her mother. "What makes it look funny?"

"Oh, I don't know," said Janie. "Patty said it was funny, so we all laughed about it."

"Yes, I know," said her mother sadly. "Louise was crying on her way home from school. I talked to her on the corner. Do you think you were kind in hurting Louise?"

Janie felt ashamed and dropped her eyes. She knew she had been unkind.

"I thought her haircut was very lovely," Janie's mother continued. "Perhaps Patty was jealous. In any case, do you like being laughed at?"

"No," was all Janie could say. She felt like crying, too.

"Well, then," said her mother, "let's not forget that Jesus wants us to love others the way we love ourselves. Love is kind. People who love try not to hurt one another."

Do you know what Janie did? She went and told Louise that her hair was nice. She was sorry she had made fun of Louise.

Let's talk about this: How were the girls at school unkind to Louise? What makes us unkind to some people? Who wants us to love other people the way we love ourselves? What kind words could the girls have said to Louise? Let's say the Bible verse together and then try to remember it.

Bible reading for older children and grownups: 1 Corinthians 13:4-7.

Let us pray for a more loving and kind heart: Dear Father in heaven, we are often thoughtless and unkind to others. Please forgive us for Jesus' sake. We know that He died also for these sins. Help us to be more loving so that we will be more kind. In Jesus' name we ask this. Amen.

*Give, not grudgingly or because you
    have to.* 2 Corinthians 9:7

What Kind of Giver Are You?

Jimmy wasn't a cheerful giver. He always wanted his gifts back. He gave Bobby a rubber ball. After a while he said, "I want it back." His giving made him unhappy, because he really didn't want to give. Sometimes his little friends would not give his gifts back. That made Jimmy very unhappy. He would even scream and fight to get them back.

Jerry was different. He liked to give things to other people. They said he was a generous boy. Jerry saw that his giving made others happy. It made him happy, too.

In Sunday school, Jimmy and Jerry heard about the children in Africa who are afraid of God. Their teacher said:

252

"You don't have to give anything, but all those who want to may bring some money next Sunday to help send more missionaries to Africa. The missionaries will tell the children in Africa about Jesus and His love."

That week Jerry asked his mother if he could sell one of his puppies. He wanted to bring a dollar for the missionaries. When the neighbor heard what Jerry wanted to do with the money, he gave Jerry *ten* dollars for the puppy.

The next Sunday morning, Jimmy brought only the nickel which his mother gave him for Sunday school. But Jerry brought the whole ten dollars he got for his puppy. Now, who do you think was the happier boy? Oh, Jerry was. He could hardly wait to get to Sunday school.

The Bible says, "God loves a cheerful giver." He doesn't want us to give as though we *had* to, but because we *want* to. And God says that when we want to, He will help us. The more we give, the more He will give to us. Isn't that exciting?

Let's talk about this: Why wasn't Jimmy a happy giver? What kind of giver does God want us to be? Let's say the Bible verse together. Why did Jerry sell one of his puppies? How did God bless Jerry? Who was the happier boy, Jimmy or Jerry? Why?

Bible reading for older children and grownups: 2 Corinthians 9:6-8.

Let us pray together: Dear God, we thank You for the many gifts You give to us every day. We thank You especially for Jesus and His love. Make us willing and cheerful givers so that we will gladly share with others what You have given to us. In Jesus' name we ask this. Amen.

*Jesus said, If two of you will agree on anything
that you will ask, it will be done for you
by My Father in heaven.* Matthew 18:19

Praying Together Helps

"Della, you ask Daddy to have a picnic tomorrow," said her brother Bob.

"No, you ask him," said Della.

"Let's both ask him," said Bob.

So they both asked their father to have a picnic. When their father saw that they both wanted very much to have a picnic, he said, "Well, if you both want it, maybe we can." They were glad.

We can talk that way to God, our Father in heaven, too. When you ask God for something, He hears you, and when I talk to God, he hears me, too. But there are some things that many Christians want. If we will go together in our prayer, even if there are only two of us, Jesus says that God will listen and will answer our prayer.

What are some things we all want? We want to be loved, we want to be happy, we want to be more like Jesus, we want

254

other people to learn about Him! Let's pray for that together, and our Father in heaven will give us what we want.

Are there some other things that you want very much? Jesus said, "If two of you will agree on anything that you will ask, it shall be done for you by My Father in heaven." Isn't that a wonderful promise? Just get someone to pray with you for what you want, and you'll see.

Let's talk about this: Why did Bob and Della both ask their father for a picnic? What did Jesus say would happen if two of His friends would ask His Father anything? What are some things nearly all Christians want? What are some things our family wants? Let us pray for them today. (Here the members of the family may each say a sentence prayer.)

Bible reading for older children and grownups: Matthew 18:19, 20.

Let us pray: Thank You, dear Father in heaven, for promising to do what Your children all want. We all want what Jesus wants, so please make us more like Him. Please keep us as Your children for Jesus' sake. Amen.

This woman was full of good works. Acts 9:36

Are We Full of Good Works?

Dorcas was dead, and many people were crying. Most of them were widows. Widows are women whose husbands have died. Most of the widows had children to feed. Dorcas helped them. She made dresses and coats for them. That's why they loved her. But now she was dead.

Some of her friends told Peter that she was dead. Peter was one of the twelve disciples of Jesus. Peter came and prayed to Jesus. He asked Jesus to make Dorcas alive again.

255

Jesus answered Peter's prayer. He made Dorcas alive and well again. She opened her eyes. When she saw Peter, she sat up.

Dorcas' friends were very happy when they saw her alive again, especially the widows whom she had helped. "She was full of good works," they said. Wouldn't we like to have people say that about us?

How did Dorcas get to be full of good works? She loved Jesus, and every day she tried to do as much good as she could. Maybe the first day nobody noticed, nor the second day either. But by and by everybody noticed that she was helping people. That's why they said, "She was full of good works."

Can people say that we are full of good works? That depends on whether we are helpful to others. How many good deeds have we been doing for others? How kind and helpful are we? Jesus wants us to be *full* of good works. Do you know a good time to start doing good works? Today. And do you know where? Wherever you are.

Let's talk about good works: What happened to Dorcas? Why were the people sorry? Whom did they tell? What did Peter do? What was said about Dorcas? How did she get to be "full of good works"? How can we become full of good works? When is it a good time to start doing good works?

Older children and grownups may now read the story of Dorcas: Acts 9:36-42.

Let us pray together: Dear Father in heaven, You have been so good to us. We thank You especially for sending Jesus to save us. Please teach us to do what we can for other people. Show us how to start in our own home and with our friends and neighbors. We want to be "full of good works" as Dorcas was, for the sake of Jesus, our Lord and Savior. Amen.

256

Be of good cheer. Matthew 9:2

How Cheerful Are You?

Everybody called her Grandma Sunshine. She had fallen down some steps and had broken her back. She was in the hospital a long time with a cast around her body. Still she would smile and say to others, "Cheer up." She was a very cheerful person.

In the same room was a lady who didn't know what was wrong with her. She was there just for a checkup. In a few days she would get to go home. But still she was worrying and complaining. She didn't like the room, and the bed was too hard, and the food was no good, and the nurses weren't nice to her, she said. The nurses called her Grumpy.

Why was Grandma Sunshine always ready to smile, even though her back hurt very much? Why didn't she complain about being in the hospital a long time? Because she knew that Jesus loved her and that she was one of God's dear children. She was also thankful for what people did for her.

Even when they are well, children often grumble and complain instead of being cheerful. But Jesus gives us a reason for being happy even when we are sick. "Be of good cheer," He said to a crippled man. Some friends had carried the man to Jesus because he couldn't walk.

Do you know why we can be happy, no matter what happens to us? Jesus told the crippled man, "Your sins are all forgiven." That's the main reason for being happy. And *our* sins are all forgiven, too, because Jesus paid for them. So "be of good cheer." Be cheerful. God loves you.

Let's talk about this: What did people call the lady with the broken back? Why? How did the other lady show that she wasn't happy? Why was Grandma Sunshine always

257

ready to smile? What did Jesus once tell a crippled man? What is the best reason for being cheerful all the time?

Bible reading for older children and grownups: Matthew 9:1-7.

Let us pray: Dear Jesus, how glad we are that You forgive all sins and that You are God. Help us to remember this so that we will be cheerful even when things don't seem right. Amen.

Lord, You have the words
of eternal life. John 6:68

Our Heavenly Map

When people are driving on a long trip, they often look at a map. Do you know why? They want to know which road to take to get to where they want to go. The map directs them. It shows them the way.

We all want to get to heaven. But not everybody knows the way. In the story called *This Way to Heaven* little Jimmy Wheeler asked a man standing by a church door, "Mister, is this the way to heaven?"

Our church teaches us the way to heaven when it teaches us the Bible. The Bible is like a map. The Bible says that Jesus is the only Way to heaven, and all who believe in Jesus and follow Him are on the right road. He is the Road that will take us to heaven.

A map not only shows the way to get somewhere; it also shows what we will see along the way. It shows the towns we must pass and the bridges we must cross and the mountains and lakes we will see. A good map also shows the detours we must take so we won't get lost or stuck in a new road.

In all these ways the Bible is like a map. Through it Jesus

258

will direct our way so that we won't get lost. That is why we need to keep on studying our Bible. It tells us how to follow Jesus in order to get to heaven. His words are the words of eternal life.

Let's talk about this: What does a driver often read on a long trip? Why? In what way is the Bible like a map? What does the Bible say is the only way to heaven? What did Peter say to Jesus in our Bible verse? Where can we find the words of Jesus? How will studying the Bible help us along the way?

Bible reading for older children and grownups: John 6:62-69.

Let us pray: Dear Jesus, we are thankful that we have learned that You are the Way to heaven. Keep us close to You on the way so that we will not get lost on wrong roads. We ask this as Your dear children. Amen.

Tomorrow will take care of itself. Matthew 6:34

Don't Worry About Tomorrow

One evening Martin Luther was looking out of a window in his house. In a tree nearby he saw a little bird getting ready for the night. "Look," he said, "how the little bird teaches us to trust in God. He takes hold of his twig, tucks his head under his wing, and goes to sleep. He lets God think and care for him."

Even children often worry about tomorrow. They wonder what they'll get to do, or whether they'll have good grades in school, or how they can become somebody's best friend, or what people will think about them.

Jesus once told us to look at the birds. They don't worry about tomorrow. They don't even work, and still God feeds them. "Are you not worth much more than they?" asked Jesus.

Jesus wants people to work. The Bible says, "If anyone will not work, neither should he eat." God wants children to grow up learning how to work. He does not bless lazy people. But He tells us not to *worry* about our work, or about anything else. He loves us and will take care of us when we trust in Him.

"Only believe," said Jesus to a man who was worried that his little girl was dead. Jesus made the little girl alive. All we have to do is trust in Jesus. Then everything will turn out all right. Don't worry.

Let's talk about this: What did Martin Luther see outside of his window one evening? How did the little bird go to sleep? About what do children sometimes worry? About what do you think older people worry? Why did Jesus tell us not to worry about food and clothes? How do we know that He wants us to work, even though He doesn't want us to worry? What did Jesus tell Jairus when his little girl died? That's all we have to do, too.

Bible reading for older children and grownups: Matthew 6:24-34.

Let us pray for a trusting heart: Dear Lord Jesus, help us to trust in You so that we need never worry. Teach us that tomorrow will take care of itself if only we will believe in You. Amen.

Seek, and you will find. Matthew 7:7

Pray and Work

Did you ever watch a chicken hunt for something to eat? It often stands and scratches the ground. It scratches the grass and stones away. When it sees something to eat, it picks it up. Chickens scratch for a living.

God wants to give us blessings, but He wants us to work for them. Jesus told us to pray for daily bread, but the bread doesn't just drop into our laps. No, God wants most people to work for a living. They must earn money in order to buy what they need.

Even when Jesus talked about God's love, He told us to go after it. "Seek, and you will find it," He said. We are to hunt for God's blessings. God wants to give them to us, but we must pray and work in order to get them.

This is the way God's plan works: He wants us to know more about Him, but we have to study the Bible. He wants us to have His forgiveness and love, but we, too, must want it. He is willing to make us more like Jesus, but we have to learn His ways of doing things and then follow them.

Remember that Jesus said, "Seek, and you will find."

Let's talk about this: Why does God want us to hunt for His gifts? What if we seek something that God does not want us to have? Why will God always help us find what is

261

best for us? Where must we look for the promises of God's love and forgiveness? If we ask God for something and really want it, what will we do besides pray? (We will try to get it, and when we try real hard, God will give it to us if it is good for us.)

Older children and grownups may now read: Matthew 13:45, 46.

Let us pray together: Dear Father in heaven, thank You for the promise that we will find Your blessings if we will look for them and work to get them. Lead us to ask for those things which You want us to have, and help us to find those things when we look for them. This we ask in Jesus' name. Amen.

Be glad in the Lord always. Philippians 4:4

A Boy Who Was Always Happy

A woman was coming down the sidewalk, pushing a wheel chair. In it sat a little boy who couldn't walk. He couldn't even move his hands very much. He had had polio. But he was smiling all the time.

"Look at that boy; he's always smiling," said Allan.

"I'd cry if I couldn't walk," said his sister Margie.

"But he's doing right by smiling," said Allan. "Don't you remember what our minister said about being happy all the time? 'Be glad in the Lord always.' That's a Bible verse."

"But how can I be happy if I don't feel happy?" asked Margie, and she sounded as though she were about to cry over that.

"We can remember how Jesus was nailed on the cross for us," said Allan. "That shows how much He loves us. Jesus makes people happy even when they can't walk."

262

"I guess I could be happy even if I were crippled, if Jesus wanted me to be," said Margie after a while.

"But when we can run and play and work, we should REALLY be glad," said Allan. "And don't forget, Jesus is going to take us to heaven."

So Allan and Margie were both glad in the Lord. And the next day they went to visit the boy in the wheel chair. They wanted to tell him that he had helped them to be happy.

Let's talk about this: How did the boy in the wheel chair show that he was happy? Do you think you could smile if you were crippled? What are some of the good things we would still have? What blessings do we have which the crippled boy didn't have? What does the Bible verse tell all of us? Why can we always be happy when we belong to Jesus?

Bible reading for older children and grownups: Philippians 4:4-7.

Let's pray to God together: Dear God, thank You for the good arms and legs You have given us, and for all Your other blessings. We thank You most of all for loving us and saving us and letting us be Your children. Make us always to be happy in Your kingdom and belong to You. We ask this in Jesus' name. Amen.

Peter said, Lord, You know
all things. John 21:17

Jesus Knows Everything

One day Jesus asked Peter, "Do you love Me?" Three times Jesus asked him this question. The third time Peter said, "Lord, You know all things. You know that I love You." Jesus did know that Peter loved Him. He knows everything. Isn't that wonderful? It may be scary, too. If Jesus knows everything, He knows all the bad things we think.

Mary didn't like her teacher. "I hope my teacher dies soon; then I can have a new teacher," she wished. Mary would never say such things, but she was thinking them. People around her didn't know what she was thinking, but Jesus knew.

Jesus knows everything. He knows the bad things we say and do and even those we only think. He knows all about us. But still He loves us. He forgives all our sins all the time because He loves us so much. He even suffered and died on a cross to save us from being punished for what we do wrong.

And Jesus knows when we really love Him, even when it doesn't look as if we did. Jimmy wanted to please Jesus, so he tried to be kind to his little brother. He reached into the cupboard to get a glass. He wanted to give his little brother a drink. The glass fell and broke. His mother became angry. She didn't know why Jimmy had broken the glass, but Jesus knew.

We're glad that Jesus knows everything.

Let's talk this over: What question did Jesus ask Peter three times? What did Peter say the third time? Why is it scary to think about that? Would we want our minister to

264

know everything we think? Why is God always willing to forgive us our sins? Why are we glad that Jesus knows everything? Let's say the Bible verse together.

Bible reading for older children and grownups: John 21:14-17.

Let us pray together: Dear Lord, please forgive us for not always showing that we love You. Help us to think and talk and act the way You want us to, because we love You and want to love You more. Amen.

See what love the Father has given us, that we should be called the children of God. 1 John 3:1

Adopted Children of God

Little Jerry's parents were often drunk. The result was that they didn't take care of him very well. When he was still a tiny baby, some neighbors heard him crying and called the police. He was all alone in the house and was hungry.

The police found Jerry's parents in a tavern. For not taking care of their baby they had to go to a judge. The judge told them that he was willing to adopt their baby, so they gave their baby to the judge.

For a long time the judge and his wife were afraid to tell Jerry that he was adopted. They thought he wouldn't like them as much if they told him he was adopted. But one day Jerry found out. Some children at school told him that the judge was not his real father. Jerry thought about that all day.

In the evening Jerry said to the judge, "You love me a lot, don't you?" "We do," said the judge, "but what makes you say that?" "Well," said Jerry, "you made me your son even though I really wasn't your son. You didn't have to do that." Jerry was right. People love adopted children as much as they would love their real children.

One day the disciple John thought about God adopting people as His children. God didn't have to. So John said, "See what love the Father has given us, that we should be called the children of God."

The Bible says, "We are all the children of God by faith in Christ Jesus." In another place it says, "As many as received Him, to all who believed in Him, He gave power to become the children of God." In other words, when we are willing to have Jesus as our Savior, God adopts us and calls us His children. He does this for Jesus' sake.

Think of how much God loves us by making us His children! Think of how wonderful it is to be one of His very own dear children! The newspapers often print pictures of children who belong to a king, and people get excited when they see these children. But we are children of God. Never forget that.

Let's talk about this: Whose son did Jerry become when he was adopted? Why did the judge and his wife adopt Jerry? What did Jerry say when he found out that the judge had adopted him? Whom does God adopt as His children? Why is God willing to make us His children? How ought we to feel about this?

Bible reading for older children and grownups: 1 John 3:1-3.

Let us thank God together: Dear Father in heaven, how glad we are that You have adopted us as Your children! How much You must love us! Keep us as Your children, and help us to show our thanks by good behavior. We ask this for the sake of Jesus, our Savior. Amen.

266

*I will fear no evil; for Thou art
with me.* Psalm 23:4

How to Get Real Brave

Two boys were reading about Elijah and how he was taken up into heaven in a wagon of fire. They talked about the wagon and how it must have looked. They wondered about the horses which had pulled it.

"I'd be afraid to ride in a wagon like that, wouldn't you?" said one of the boys.

The other boy answered, "I wouldn't be afraid; not if God were driving."

People who believe in Jesus know that God loves them. They say what King David said in Psalm 23: "The Lord is my Shepherd." Jesus is like a good shepherd, who takes very good care of his lambs and sheep. He doesn't let anything hurt them.

Do you know the rest of Psalm 23? In it King David also said, "I will fear no evil; for Thou art with me." People who belong to Jesus and stay close to Him can always be brave. They never have to be afraid of anything bad happening to them. The Bible says that everything turns out good for those who love Jesus. Jesus lets only good things happen to those who love and follow Him.

Now, we wouldn't ever be afraid of something if we knew it couldn't hurt us, would we? And when we know that something is good, it makes us happy instead of afraid. So, to be real brave and happy, don't forget that Jesus is with us all the time and loves us very much. He even died on a cross for us. Don't forget that.

Let's talk about this: Why is Jesus called the Good Shepherd? Who are His lambs and sheep? How can we keep

267

Jesus near us? Why can we be real brave when He is near us? Who can say the Bible verse from memory?

All who can may now say or read: Psalm 23.

Let us pray together: Dear Lord Jesus, our Savior and Shepherd, we know that You are also with us and that we belong to You. Help us to remember this every day so that we will never be afraid of anything bad happening to us. Make us brave and happy, like David was, and keep us close to You always. Amen.

Be happy always. 1 Thessalonians 5:16

When to Be Happy

Little Sammy had to wear braces on his legs in order to walk. He had had polio. Even though he fell often, he went to school.

One day at school Sammy fell at the top of the steps and rolled down. The teacher was very frightened. She ran to him and said, "Sammy, are you hurt?" Sammy smiled up at her and said, "No, I've learned how to fall."

Sammy had learned how to be happy even when things didn't go right. He could smile even when he fell and hurt himself. In our Bible verse God tells us to be happy all the time. No matter what happens to us, we can be happy if we will remember how much God loves us. He loved us so much that He sent His Son Jesus to save us. Because of that, we are His own dear children.

Have you learned to be happy always? Can you smile when you can't have your way? Or do you curl up your lip and cry over every little thing? Remember, God wants us to be happy all the time. He expects us to be happy because Jesus has made us God's children. That's why a real little girl used to pray, "Dear Jesus, don't let me cry any more." God doesn't want His children to be cry-babies. When you feel like crying, start thinking of how good God is to you.

Let's talk about this: Can people be happy even when they have to wear braces on their legs? What is the best reason we have for always being happy? How do we know that God loves us? Why doesn't God want His children to be cry-babies? Let's say the Bible verse together.

Bible reading for older children and grownups: 1 Thessalonians 5:14-23.

Let us pray together: Dear God, we are glad that Jesus has made us Your children. Forgive us for not always being as happy as we ought to be, and help us to smile even when things don't seem right. We know that You love us, and that's reason enough for us to be happy always. Amen.

God for Christ's sake has forgiven you. Ephesians 4:32c

Why Our Sins Are Forgiven

Johnny was looking at a picture book of India. There was a big, fat, ugly idol on one page, and some people were bowing down to him. Others were lighting sticks for him, and some were giving him food and money.

"Mother, why do they do that?" asked Johnny.

"Because they want the idol to forgive their sins and be good to them," his mother told him.

"We don't have to do that to have our sins forgiven, do we?" asked Billy. "We don't have to burn candles or pay God for what we do wrong, do we?"

"No," said his mother, "God is much better to us than that

269

idol is to his people. We don't need to pay anything to have our sins forgiven. But Somebody did have to pay for them."

"I know," said Johnny. "Jesus paid for our sins."

"I'm glad that you know this, Johnny," said his mother. "And we love Jesus for having done this for us, don't we?"

"Yes," said Johnny, "and for letting us know about it so we don't pay a fat idol. He couldn't forgive us anyhow."

"That's right," said Johnny's mother. " 'God for Christ's sake has forgiven you.' That's what the Bible says."

Let's think this over: What were the people in the picture giving to a big, fat idol? Why do people give presents to idols? Who has paid for all sins? How did Jesus pay for all sins? For whose sake does God forgive us? How can we show our thanks?

Bible reading for older children and grownups: Psalm 85.

Let us pray: Thank You, dear heavenly Father, for loving and forgiving us. Teach us to help the missionaries who preach the good news about the way sins are forgiven. Help people all over the world to know that Jesus is their Savior so that they will love and trust in Him. We ask this in Jesus' name. Amen.

Love your neighbor as yourself. Romans 13:9

The Golden Rule

Little Margie was always running into the house to tell her mother what her brother was doing. "Ronnie pushed me," "Ronnie threw my doll on the ground," "Ronnie won't let me swing," she would say. She wanted her mother to scold Ronnie.

One day Margie's mother took a big sheet of paper and drew a line down the center. "First tell me all the things
270

you would like Ronnie to do," she said. So Margie told her many things, and her mother wrote them on one side of the paper. "I want him to let me swing, and I want him to let me go along to the store, and I want to play with his ball, and I want him to read me the funnies, and I don't want him to hit me," and on and on she went.

"Now tell me the things you want to do for Ronnie," said her mother. At first Margie couldn't think of anything. "But the Bible says, 'Love your neighbor as yourself,'" her mother told her. "God wants us to love other people just as much as we love ourselves. We don't want others to hurt us, so we won't want to hurt them if we love them. And if we want others to be kind to us, we will be kind to them if we love them. Jesus said, 'Whatever we want others to do for us, that we should do for them.'"

Now Margie and her mother began to put down on the other side of the paper what Margie could do for her brother. When the list on one side was just as long as the other, her mother said, "Let's remember that Jesus wants us to love Ronnie the way we want Ronnie to love us." After that, Margie and Ronnie got along much better, and Margie was a much happier girl.

Let's talk about this: What do you think was the main reason why Margie was a tattletale? What are some of the things we like to have people do for us? Do we ever like to have someone hurt us or say mean things about us? What is the Golden Rule that the Bible tells us to follow? Who is our neighbor?

Bible reading for older children and grownups: Romans 13:8-10.

Let us pray: Thank You, dear Jesus, for loving us more than You loved Yourself. Help us to love You by loving other people the way we love ourselves. Amen.

271

To do good forget not. Hebrews 13:16

Something to Remember

Charles had a birthday, and he got a dollar from his uncle, a cowboy suit from his parents, a ball from his neighbors. It was fun having a birthday and getting things.

The next day Fred had a birthday. Fred was the crippled boy who lived down the street. He sat in a wheel chair most of the time. Charles took his dollar and bought Fred a book about the Sugar Creek Gang. He knew that Fred loved the Sugar Creek Gang books.

Fred's eyes popped wide open when he saw what the present was! "Boy, thanks, thanks a lot," he said. Then Charles knew it was true. "It's more fun to give something than to get something."

The prophet Elijah once came to a widow. The widow had only a little food left in her house. After that was gone, she thought she would have to die. But Elijah asked her to give him something to eat. It was a test for her. She gave her food to him, because she believed what Elijah told her about God. And for a long time God kept giving her enough food for her family.

The Bible says, "To do good forget not." This means, "Don't forget to do good." In another place it says, "As we have opportunity, let us do good to all people." God is pleased when we do good things because we love Him.

Let's talk about this: Was Charles happy when he received gifts on his birthday? What made him feel even better? How did God bless the widow who gave food to His servant Elijah? What does the Bible tell us not to forget? For whom does God want us to do good?

Older children and grownups may now read: 1 Timothy 6:17-19.

Let us pray: Dear heavenly Father, You give us so much every day. Please forgive us for ever being selfish, and make us willing to do what we can for others. In Jesus' name we pray this. Amen.

Jesus has the power to forgive sins. Matthew 9:6

The Load Only Jesus Can Lift

"My, isn't he strong!" said the people as they watched the strong man in the circus. The strong man asked two other men to come and lift one of his weights. They couldn't lift it. Then he took one weight in one hand and another in the other hand. He lifted them both high above his head.

But there is a load that the strong man could not lift. The load is sin. The only One who can lift it is Jesus.

One day a sick man was brought to Jesus. His friends

273

wanted to help him get well. But the man wanted something else first. He wanted his sins to be forgiven. His sins were like a heavy load on him. So when Jesus saw what was bothering the sick man, He said, "Your sins are forgiven." And to show that He had the power to forgive sins, He told the man, "Pick up your bed and walk." Right away the sick man could do it.

Did you ever notice that when you have done something bad, you don't feel very good? It bothers you and keeps bothering you. It is like a heavy load on you. But when you tell your father or mother you are sorry, and you ask Jesus to forgive you, then you feel good again. The load is gone.

Jesus is able to forgive sins. He paid for all sins by dying on a cross. That is why the Bible says, "Jesus has the power to forgive sins."

Let's talk about this: Why didn't the sick man ask his friends to forgive his sins? Why did they bring him to Jesus? What did Jesus say to the man? How did Jesus show that He has the power to forgive sins? How can we get rid of all our sins? Let's remember the Bible verse and say it together.

Older children and grownups may now read: Matthew 9:1-8.

Let's ask Jesus to forgive us our sins, too: Dear Lord Jesus, please forgive all the wrong things we have done. Do not let our sins bother us like a heavy load, but take them all away. We know You can, because You are God's Son and have the power to forgive sins. Thank You, dear Jesus, for loving us. Amen.

You will see Jesus . . . coming in the clouds of heaven. Matthew 26:64

The Biggest Surprise Ever

"Will that ever be a surprise!" said little Eddie when he came home from church one day.

"What will be a surprise?" asked his dad. He had stayed home that day and was reading the funny papers.

"When all the people of the world will see Jesus coming in the clouds of heaven. Jesus said they would. He said it when He was standing in front of Caiaphas."

Eddie's dad didn't believe him, but Eddie was right. Caiaphas did not like Jesus. He wanted Jesus to be dead. He asked Jesus, "Are You the Savior whom God promised to send?" Jesus said, "Yes, I am. Someday you will see Me coming in the clouds of heaven."

Caiaphas didn't believe Jesus either. Lots of people don't believe that Jesus is coming again. But Jesus said He would, and everybody will see Jesus coming. We will see Him coming in the clouds, too.

If we have asked Jesus to be our Savior, we will be glad when He comes. He will not come to punish us but to take us to heaven. That will be like all the Christmases we ever had and all the Easters put together, only much better. It will be the most wonderful day that ever happened. That's why little Eddie was happy.

Let's think about this: Who is going to be coming again in the clouds? Why will this be a surprise? Jesus said that Caiaphas would see Him. How will Caiaphas feel when he sees Jesus coming? Who else will see Jesus coming in the clouds? How will the people who love Jesus feel? What will happen to those who asked Jesus to be their Savior?

275

Do you want Jesus to be your Savior? He wants to take us all to heaven.

Bible reading for older children and grownups: Luke 21:25-36.

Let us pray: Dear Lord Jesus, we are glad that You are coming again, because we know that You love us and have saved us and will take us to heaven. Please help everyone to believe You so that they will get ready and not be surprised when You come. Amen.

Blessed are all they that put their trust in Jesus. Psalm 2:12

We Trust in Jesus

Tim and his father were out walking in a woods. They came to a little river that had no bridge. Someone had put a long log across the water. It could be used to get across the water.

Tim was afraid to walk on the log. He was afraid he would fall into the water. But when his father said, "I'll carry you across," then Tim wasn't afraid any more. He trusted his father.

Just like Tim trusted his father, so we can trust Jesus. He is the Son of God and can do anything. He is the Ruler of the world and can help us in any trouble.

When Tim's father carried him across the river, Tim hung on for dear life. He was both glad and scared. He was glad to have his father's strong and loving arms around him. But he held on tightly and was a little worried.

Like Tim, we need to hold on to Jesus so that we will not slip away from Him. Our Bible verse says, "Blessed are

276

all they that put their trust in Him." This means, we will be happy and safe in His loving arms if we will let Him carry us across dangers all the way to heaven.

Let's see what we have learned: What was Tim afraid to do by himself? When was Tim not afraid to cross the river on a log? What does it mean to trust someone? How did Tim trust his father? Why can we trust that Jesus will help and save us? What does the Bible verse say about all who put their trust in Jesus?

Bible reading for older children and grownups: Psalm 46.

Let us pray together: Dear Lord Jesus, please hold us close to You in Your strong and loving arms every day. Then we know that we will be safe and will get to where You want us to go. We love You. Amen.

*Faith comes by hearing . . . the Word
of God.* Romans 10:17

How People Become Christians

Chief Kawa took his bow and arrow. He was going to kill the missionary. He walked quietly to some bushes behind the place where the missionary was talking.

Nobody saw Kawa. He didn't want to be seen. But while Kawa got ready to shoot, he heard the missionary tell a story. It was the story of the lost sheep. "God is like a shepherd," said the missionary. "He loves His sheep. He does not want to lose any. So He sent His Son Jesus to save His sheep."

Because Kawa heard those words, he did not shoot the arrow. He hid it in the bushes and listened. When the sermon was over, Kawa went to the missionary. "Tell me more about Jesus," he said. Later Kawa became a Christian. He believed that Jesus was his Savior, and he loved Him. Then Kawa also tried to please Jesus.

How did all this happen? It happened when Kawa heard some preaching. If Kawa had not heard about Jesus, he would never have loved Him. By hearing the Word of God the chief began to believe that Jesus was his Savior. He also loved Jesus and wanted to be one of His people. That is what is meant by faith.

To get faith and to keep on having faith, we must hear and learn the Word of God. "Faith comes by hearing . . . the Word of God." We help send missionaries so that others, too, will learn to love Jesus by hearing about Him.

Let's talk about this: What did Kawa want to do? Why didn't he shoot the missionary? How did Kawa become a Christian? What does it mean to believe in Jesus? How did we get our faith? Why are we glad to help missionaries?

278

Bible reading for older children and grownups: Romans 10:14-17.

Let us pray: Dear Father in heaven, we are glad that we can hear and learn Your words in the Bible. Give us a strong faith in Jesus and all that You have said. Bless all preaching and teaching of Your Word so that many more people will hear and learn about Jesus and will love and trust Him, too. We ask this in Jesus' name. Amen.

Bless the Lord, your God, for the good land
which He has given you. Deuteronomy 8:10

The DP Family

"Dad, what are DP's?" asked Billy. A DP family had moved into the house next door.

"DP's are displaced persons. They are people who had to leave their homes in a faraway land," said Billy's father.

"Why did they have to leave their homes? Did they do something bad?" asked Billy.

"No," said his father, "there was a war, and some enemies took their homes."

"People in our country are safe, aren't they?" said Billy.

"Yes," said his father, "as long as God protects us. He

has been extra good to the people in our country. Most of us have a home, and most people have jobs, and almost everybody has more than enough to eat. Do you know what Moses told the people of Israel to do when God gave them a home in the good country of Canaan?"

Billy shook his head.

"Bless the Lord, your God, for the good land which He has given you," Billy's father told him. "Moses knew that there were plenty of good things to eat in the land of Canaan."

"Yeah," said Billy, "in some countries the children have to go to bed hungry every day because they don't get enough to eat." He had heard this in Sunday school.

"That's right," said his father, "and that's not the only reason why we ought to do what the Bible verse says: 'Bless the Lord, your God, for the good land which He has given you!' Can you think of another?"

Billy thought for a while. "I know," he said. "In our country we can have our own church, and we can go when we want to."

"That's right," said Billy's father, "and that's one of the best reasons for thanking God for our country."

Let's talk about this: Why did the DP's leave their home in a faraway country? Why do some people in other countries go to bed hungry? In what ways is God extra good to us and the people in our country? Who can say the Bible verse from memory?

Bible reading for older children and grownups: Deuteronomy 8:5-20.

Let us bless God: We praise and thank You, God, for the good land which You have given to us. Help us to show our thanks by gladly obeying Your commandments. In Jesus' name we ask this. Amen.

280

It is a good thing to give thanks
to the Lord. Psalm 92:1

Giving God Thanks

A Sunday school class made up a litany one Sunday morning. A litany is a prayer in which one person says the first part of a sentence and all the others say the second part. This one was a prayer of thanks. It went something like this:

For sending Jesus to be our Savior,
Dear God, we are thankful.

For the Holy Bible,
Dear God, we are thankful.

For parents who teach us about Jesus and His love,
Dear God, we are thankful.

For our church and our church school,
Dear God, we are thankful.

For making us Your children,
Dear God, we are thankful.

For our family and our home,
Dear God, we are thankful.

For Your love and care and blessings,
Dear God, we are thankful.

The Bible says, "It is a good thing to give thanks to the Lord." It is good because He deserves to be thanked for being kind to us every day. It is also good for us. It makes us happy when we think of how good God is to us, and when we praise and thank Him.

We thank God when we pray and when we sing — at home and in church. Of course, we can thank Him without speaking. But what if we could not speak or sing to God

281

at all! How sad we would be! "It is a good thing to give thanks unto the Lord." So let's do it often, alone and together, at home and at church.

Some questions to think about: What are some of the things for which God deserves to be thanked by all of us? What does our Bible verse say about giving thanks to the Lord? Why is it good for us to give thanks to the Lord?

Bible reading for older children and grownups: Psalm 92:1-5.

Let us give thanks to the Lord: Dear God, we want to thank You for all that You have done for us: for making the world so beautiful, for sending Jesus to die for us on a cross, and for loving us as Your children. How good You are to all of us, dear Lord. Help us to show our love to You every day, for Jesus' sake. Amen.

Freely you have received,
  freely give. Matthew 10:8

God's Gifts Are Free

Once a rosebush and a snail lived together in the corner of a garden. The rosebush was happy all day long. It was thankful to God for the fresh air and the warm sun and the good rain. Every day it grew a little more, and soon it was covered with roses. The sweet and beautiful flowers praised God and made people happy.

The snail lived underneath the rosebush. It liked to stay in the shadows and do nothing. When anyone came near, it would crawl into its shell as if to say, "I'm not interested in anybody else."

One day the snail looked up and said to the rosebush,

282

"You are foolish for always giving people your roses." The rosebush smiled back and said, "How can I help giving the things which God gives to me?"

God's children are always receiving His gifts of love free of charge. Every day they receive His forgiveness and His Spirit. They also receive His loving care and their daily food. Why shouldn't they gladly share God's gifts with others, especially the sweet story of Jesus and what He has done for the whole world?

Jesus said, "Freely you have received, freely give." Let us gladly give to other people what we receive freely from God. Then we will be more like a rose than a snail.

Let's talk about this: What do rosebushes give to people? Who gives roses to the rosebushes? Why does God want us to be like a rosebush and not like a snail? What are some of the things God gives to us every day without making us pay for them? What is the best gift God gives to us all the time? How can we give this gift to others?

Bible reading for older children and grownups: Luke 6:30-38.

Let us pray together: Dear Jesus, we thank You for giving us Your love and blessings freely every day. Help us to share them by giving them freely to others. Amen.

For you is born this day in the city of David a Savior,
which is Christ, the Lord. Luke 2:11

The Most Wonderful Night

Everything was dark, but the shepherds watching their sheep near Bethlehem were used to that. Many nights had been dark and lonely for them, and they didn't expect this night to be any different. They didn't know that their nights would never have to be lonely again.

All of a sudden there was a bright light around them. The glory of God was shining down on them. At first the shepherds were terribly afraid of what might happen. Then they heard an angel talk to them. The angel said, "Do not be afraid, because I bring you good news that should make you very happy. For you a little Baby has just been born over there in Bethlehem. He is the Lord, the promised Savior. You will find the Baby lying in a manger, wrapped in baby clothes."

Then many more angels came and still more, until there were more than anybody could count. They were all praising God and singing, and I wish we could have heard that choir.

284

"Glory to God in heaven, and on earth peace, good will toward men," they sang.

When the angels had gone back to heaven, the shepherds said to one another, "Let us go to Bethlehem right away and see the Savior." So they left their sheep and hurried away. They found Mary and Joseph, and the Baby Jesus lying on some hay in a manger. How happy they were! What the angel had told them was true! God's Son, the promised Savior, had come from heaven to help them get to heaven. On the way home they told many others what they knew about the Baby Jesus.

Let's talk about this: What is the night called on which Jesus was born? Who were the first ones to hear about the coming of the Baby Jesus? How did God tell the shepherds that their Savior had come? Why did the many angels sing? Where did the shepherds find Jesus? What did the shepherds do after they had seen the Baby Jesus? Why are all Christians glad that Jesus came?

Bible reading: Luke 2:8-20.

Let us pray together:

Be near me, Lord Jesus, I ask Thee to stay
Close by me forever, and love me, I pray.
Bless all the dear children in Thy tender care,
And take us to heaven to live with Thee there.

Amen.

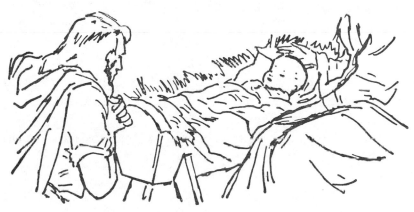

He is risen, as He said. Matthew 28:6.

The Most Wonderful Day

A long time ago, as you know, Jesus lived on this earth. After He grew up, He went from one place to the next. He told people that He was God's Son. He taught them how they could become God's children. He said that He had come to save all people from their sins.

Wherever He went, many people followed Him. They wanted to learn more about Him and His Father in heaven. They also brought their children and their sick friends to Jesus. He loved and helped them all. After a while they wanted to make Him their king.

But the wicked rulers did not love Jesus. They did not believe that He was the Savior God had promised to send. So they arrested Him and hung Him on a cross to die. The Bible tells us that Jesus let them do this to Him. He was willing to die so that His Father in heaven could forgive all the wrong things that anybody did.

Three days after Jesus was killed, the most wonderful thing happened. It was early in the morning. Soldiers were

286

guarding Jesus' grave. All at once the earth shook. A shining angel came down from heaven and rolled the stone away from the door of Jesus' grave. The soldiers fell over like dead men. When they got up, the angel and Jesus were gone.

Early that morning some women who loved Jesus came to His grave. Mary Magdalene was one of them. When the women saw that the grave was open, Mary Magdalene ran back to the city to tell the disciples. The other women went up to the grave. There, inside, they saw two angels. One of them said, "We know you are looking for Jesus. He is not here. He is risen!" Then these women hurried to Jerusalem to tell the disciples what they had seen and heard.

A little later Mary Magdalene came back to the grave alone. She was crying because she thought someone had stolen Jesus' body. All at once Jesus stood near her. Mary thought He was the man who took care of the garden. "Sir," she said, "if you have taken Jesus away, tell me where you have put Him." Jesus said, "Mary!" Then she knew it was Jesus. Jesus said to her, "Go and tell My disciples that I am alive again." Now Mary was happy. She ran to tell her friends the good news.

Let's talk about this: Why did many people want Jesus to be their king? Why did the rulers kill Jesus? What happened on the first Easter morning? What did the angel tell the women? How did Mary Magdalene know that Jesus really was alive?

Bible reading: Matthew 28:1-8.

Let us pray together: Dear Lord Jesus, please fill our hearts with true Easter joy. Help us all to believe that You are our living Savior. Live in our hearts so that we will live with You now and forever in heaven. Amen.

Index